Merrehope

Written in the Bricks

A Visual and Historical Tour of Fifteen Mississippi Hometowns

Text by Mary Carol Miller
Photographs by Mary Rose Carter

QUAIL RIDGE PRESS • BRANDON

QUAIL RIDGE PRESS
1-800-343-1583 • P. O. Box 123 • Brandon, MS 39043
e-mail: info@quailridge.com • URL: www.quailridge.com

9 8 7 6 5 4 3 2 1

Library of Congress Cataloging-in-Publication Data

Miller, Mary Carol.
    Written in the bricks : a visual and historical tour of fifteen Mississippi
hometowns / text by Mary Carol Miller ; photographs by Mary Rose
Carter.
      p. cm.
    Includes index.
    ISBN 1-893062-09-0
    1. Mississippi—History, Local. 2. Mississippi—History, Local Pictorial
works. 3. Cities and towns—Mississippi—History. 4. Cities and towns—
Mississippi—History Pictorial works.
I. Carter, Mary Rose. II. Title.
F341.M54 1999
976.2—dc21   99-39583
                                                  CIP

Book and jacket design by Cynthia Clark

Dedication

For our families: Jimmy, Emily and Jim
Michael, Claire and Hal, and Walker

and

For Rena Stott Roach and Bonnie Prince Charlie,
who started it all.

Table of Contents

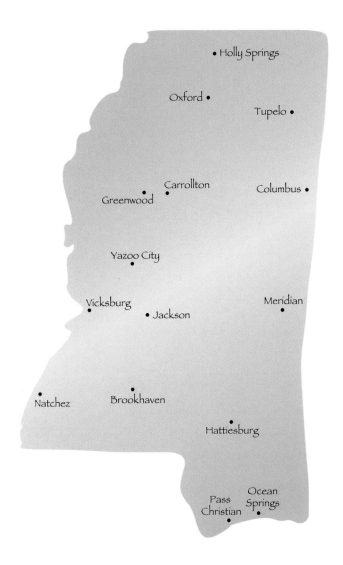

Introduction

*M*ississippi's history can't really be found in books. When it's reduced to names and dates and maps, it dries up and blows away like clouds of dust, forgotten as soon as the page is turned.

If you want to truly grasp three hundred years of this state, you have to get out and touch it. It's soaked into the dirt of the Delta and the sands of the Coast, written in the bricks of Natchez and Holly Springs and floating along the muddy currents of the Tallahatchie and the Yazoo.

Run your hands along the crumbling walls of Chalmers Institute in Holly Springs, where Mississippi's first university sprang to life, sputtered and died. A few blocks away, you can stand on the massive stone steps of Mississippi Industrial College's long-abandoned Carnegie Auditorium and try to imagine what it must have been like for a sharecropper's son to enter those doors into a world of education and hope.

Look up into the empty turrets of Ole Miss' Barnard Observatory and feel Chancellor Barnard's despair as his dreams marched away with the doomed University Greys. Or climb the makeshift staircase into the dark, echoing upper floors of Longwood and be overwhelmed by Haller Nutt's realization that this was, indeed, nothing more than "Nutt's Folly."

Wait until fall's first frost drives the snakes away and hike into the Carroll County woods which have reclaimed Greenwood Leflore's Malmaison. Mounds of bricks from the fireplaces lie where they fell as the house burned around them; the broad front steps mark the porch where the old Choctaw sat, rifle in lap, challenging his Confederate neighbors to pull the American flag down from his mansion's cupola.

Imagine Sarah Bernhardt hitting the first high note of *La Tosca* on a Meridian night in 1892, the gas lights of the Grand Opera House shining on her costume. And just picture an army of elderly matrons descending on the New Capitol, wagging their fingers under legislators' noses and daring them to even think about tearing down the Governor's Mansion. The legislators are long gone, but the Governor's Mansion still stands. If you linger in the shadow of its portico long enough, you can feel the tension between a conquered state and the country trying to reclaim it as Governor Humphreys' family was marched out of the mansion between rows of bayoneted soldiers in 1868.

Our goal in this book is to bring these Mississippi treasures to life. We have travelled the length and breadth of the state, photographing the sites and talking with the people who care for them. Many of the photos were taken on city streets, where slices of Mississippi history are wedged into modern life. Others are so far removed from the beaten path that the twentieth century fades away completely. All are inspiring in their own fashion, from the antebellum grandeur of an Auburn or an Ammadelle to the simplicity of Grace Episcopal Church or Live Oak Cemetery.

Mississippi's story is three centuries of fascinating tales, told through the homes and courthouses and bridges and dusty old ox trails. This book will guide you to the source of those stories, but don't look for true understanding on the printed page. The essence of Mississippi is in the sites themselves, reminders of who we are and where we've come from.

It's written in the bricks.

Mary Carol Miller
Mary Rose Carter
August 1999

Acknowledgments

There was a motorcycle ad in the 1960s which claimed "You meet the nicest people on a Honda." In our experience, you meet the nicest people when you start exploring Mississippi's historic architecture. There's something about showing off their hometown which just brings out the hospitable nature of Mississippians, and we have found that to be true in every part of the state. It's a rare treat indeed to wander around Yazoo City with Sam Olden or spend a spring morning with Bill Crawford and Henry Ledet in Brookhaven. Vicksburg's Old Courthouse comes to life when Gordon Cotton walks its hill with you, and Margaret Remy knows to watch your expression when she flips on the lights in Meridian's Grand Opera House, plunging you back a hundred years in a moment's time. To every one who unlocked a door or gave us a tour or passed along local lore, we are most grateful. These people and so many more have made working on this book a pleasure; they are listed by city below.

Barney and Gwen McKee of Quail Ridge Press were willing to mold our ideas for a book into reality and give them direction and impetus. They have been faithful supporters of Mississippi writers for years, and we appreciate the chance to work with a publisher who believes, as we do, that the supply of fascinating stories in Mississippi is limitless.

Ann Becker at *Mississippi Magazine* featured our articles on several of these towns over the last few years, and we have included some of the photographs from those articles in this volume. Our gratitude goes to Ann for her willingness to highlight the state's communities in print.

Special thanks go to Mark Brady and Marie Woodsack at Hasselblad Camera Repair in New Jersey, Dixie Color Lab in Memphis and Deville Camera in Jackson for their consistently outstanding work.

Near the end of a six-month odyssey of traveling, photographing and writing, Dr. Michael Wheelis and his staff at Magnolia Hill Plantation in Kingston provided us with a delightful weekend to just relax. This is the very essence of what we have tried to present in our book: Beautiful countryside, extraordinary architecture and people who know the meaning of hospitality. To Marilyn Maniscalco, Shirley Graves, Mike Lindsay and all the dogs: Thanks for reminding us of just how good life in Mississippi can get.

As always, our families were the real troupers behind this book. Jimmy and Mike have juggled their medical careers with carpools, feeding the dogs and trying to remember just exactly where their long-lost wives were on any given day. They never complained and had faith in this project even when we had some serious doubts. Our children have been magnificent through the entire process of putting a book together. Emily solved computer crises, Jim kept us laughing and Claire and Walker provided long-distance encouragement without fail. Every writer and every photographer should be blessed with such a crew.

To thank each of these individuals for their contributions would require another entire book. These are the people who made it possible and made it fun:

BROOKHAVEN: Henry Ledet, William Crawford, Tom Moak, Paul Jackson, John Lynch.

CARROLLTON: Katherine Williams, Jay Williams, Wessie and Peter Gee, Simpson Hemphill, Sam Pitner, Tim James, Pamela Lee.

COLUMBUS: Carolyn Neault, Sam Kaye, Ken P'Pool, Reverend Murray Bullock.

GREENWOOD: May Whittington, Charles E. Wright, Sara Criss, Allen Hammond, Mary Ann Shaw.

HATTIESBURG: Linda McMurtrey, John and Gwen Deakle, Joe Tatum.

HOLLY SPRINGS: Hubert McAlexander, Milton Winter, Mary Eleanor Wyatt, Chesley Thorne Smith, Jane Callicutt, Lillian Clarke, Warner Dickerson, Jim Waldon.

JACKSON: Mary Lorenz, Jody Rigby, Andrew Mattiace, Laurie McRee, Ken P'Pool, Richard Cawthon, Jimmy Love, Judy Fenter, Teresa King, Lawrence Clark.

MERIDIAN: Margaret Remy, Fonda Rush, Jessie Brewster, Sandy McLean, Eunice Slaughter, Meridian Department of Parks and Recreation.

NATCHEZ: Ron Miller, Mimi Miller, Dr. and Mrs. George Moss, Judy Braswell, Bob Dodson, Kay Nutt, Pam Woods, Debbie Chellette, Michael Wheelis, Marilyn Maniscalco, Shirley Graves, Mike Lindsay.

OCEAN SPRINGS: Bruce Tolar, Ray Bellande, Courtney Blossman, Clayton Bass, Margaret Miller, Mrs. Eads Poitevent, Barbara Delano.

OXFORD: David Sansing, Richard Howorth, Dorothy Lee Tatum, Ann Abadie, Pat Miller, Duncan Gray.

PASS CHRISTIAN: Pat Mowry, Heinz and Frances Hoffman, Reverend Chris Colby, Julia Frye.

TUPELO: Gary Carnathan, Ricky Campbell, Alice Rogers, Betty Rogers, Diana Ezell, Jess Mark, Lee Walsh.

VICKSBURG: Nancy Bell, Gordon Cotton, Sharon Humble, Mark Greenberg, Beverly Johnson, Terry Winschel.

YAZOO CITY: Sam Olden, Mary Jones, Glo Baker, Cam Seward, Katherine Merkle, A.J. Scott, Edna Strauder.

Author's Notes

$\mathcal{M}$ ississippi has hundreds of towns, and every one has a story. Weaving them all together gives us the history of our state, from the first encounters between Indian tribes and European explorers, through territorial wilderness and antebellum prosperity, war and Reconstruction, railroad riches and Depression.

It would be impossible to tell more than a fraction of those stories in one volume. We have attempted to highlight fifteen unique communities in this book, ranging from tiny Carrollton to metropolitan Jackson. In each, we emphasize historic buildings and sites to explain how that town came to be and the events that shaped it. Every corner of the state is represented in these pages, from the oldest towns along the Gulf Coast and Mississippi River to the ones which grew up overnight in the old Choctaw and Chickasaw territories and those that developed along the railroads and in the pine forests.

Some of the photos you'll see here are familiar ones like the Old Capitol and Longwood, standards in any book of Mississippi history. But many of the pictures and tales will be new to the casual observer of the state, and not all are pristine and proud. In traveling thousands of miles along Mississippi roads, we felt an urgency to document sites like Chalmers Institute, Wechsler School and Keesler Bridge; these structures are every bit as vital to who we are as a people as the finest houses in Natchez or the spots every tourist knows to visit. It is our hope that these words and pictures will pull you off the interstate to explore Mississippi and its wonderful heritage, always mindful that we have a duty to protect and preserve these reminders of our past.

Natchez

Auburn

$\mathcal{M}$ention Natchez, and the mind conjures up columns and azaleas, mansions and magnolias. The image is carefully cultivated and is accurate in its reflection of the decades when cotton built this river town into a mecca for millionaires.

Digging a bit deeper into the story of Natchez, both before and during the reign of King Cotton, reveals a more complex story. Indian massacres, decadent living, guilt-ridden nabobs and secret diaries combine to tell the tale of the oldest settlement in the lower Mississippi River Valley.

The river was the key to Natchez. French explorer Pierre Lemoyne d'Iberville's mission when he sailed into the Gulf of Mexico in 1699 was not to find beaches but to locate the mouth of the Mississippi. He accomplished that goal, traveled several hundred miles up the river, and identified the Natchez bluffs as a likely site for a French fort. In 1816, his brother, Jean Baptiste Lemoyne Bienville, returned to build the first Fort Rosalie.

The palisaded Fort Rosalie was so far removed from civilization that it was unlikely to be threatened by Spaniards or Englishmen. The only people in the area who were not subjects of King Louis XIV were the Natchez Indians, a culturally advanced tribe clustered into nine villages along St. Catherine's Creek. Relations between the French and Natchez were initially cordial, but deteriorated rapidly as the French claimed more and more of the agricultural tribe's lands.

The disputes came to a head in November, 1729. Fort Rosalie Commander D'Echepare had set his sights on White Apple Village, one of the Indians' prime farming areas, and made known his intentions to take control of

Completed in 1812, Auburn was the first of Natchez' grand Federal mansions. Dr. Stephen Duncan, the world's largest slaveholder, lived here while struggling to repatriate freed slaves to Africa.

The original village of Natchez bore not even a remote resemblance to the prosperous city it was to become—when cotton built this town into a mecca for millionaires.

its produce. The Natchez had been pushed far enough. Under the pretense of delivering poultry to the stockade, they gained entrance to the fort and massacred 250 men, women and children. Fort Rosalie was sacked and destroyed.

The triumph of the Natchez was short-lived. French forces swarmed up the river from New Orleans, overwhelming the warriors of the tribe and driving the survivors into Louisiana. By the time Fort Rosalie was reconstructed in 1732, the Natchez no longer existed as a tribe. The fort served little purpose and was skimpily garrisoned for the next thirty years. As America moved toward independence and European countries warred over their New World possessions, the area passed into the hands of the British and then the Spanish. It developed as a sanctuary for British sympathizers during the American Revolution, many arriving with large land grants from a grateful Crown. Although Spain took control in 1781, the prevailing atmosphere in Natchez was definitely English.

Natchez was formally platted as a town in 1791. At the time, most of its buildings hugged the shoreline beneath the bluffs, serving the flatboats trolling along the river. A few homes and businesses were starting to appear above the bluffs, but the village bore not even a remote resemblance to the prosperous city which it would be fifty years later. Most houses were little more than mud and log huts; the few finer houses tended to be designed along the lines of West Indian homes, with raised masonry basements supporting frame living quarters.

The first brick house to be built in Natchez belonged to Michael Solibellas, a Spaniard who had received the property at the corner of Wall and Washington Streets from the Spanish government. His lot and house were auctioned in 1798, with the dwelling described as a 50'x30' house. It was acquired by Manuel Texada for the considerable sum of $1000. Texada was a native Spaniard who had come to America to make his fortune as a lawyer, planter and tavernkeeper. He stayed on after Mississippi became a U. S. territory with Natchez as its first capital. Texada lived in the house which would bear his name and rented out the excess space to various businesses. Government and the blooming cotton economy brought increasing numbers of visitors and newcomers to Natchez, and Texada prospered by renting space in his house for the Beaumont Hotel and City Tavern, advertised as being in "a large elegant and commodious new brick house."

Texada was a respectable establishment. Those looking for rowdier entertainment needed only go a few blocks west and down the slope of Silver Street to find something quite different. "Natchez Under the Hill" was a world unto itself. This was where the paths of Natchez Trace robbers crossed the muddy footprints of rough keelboaters and gamblers. Saloons and brothels never closed and never lacked for business. Respectable Natchezians braced themselves when they had to run this gauntlet of iniquity to conduct business along the wharves; one horrified visitor described Natchez Under the Hill: "For the size of it, there is not, perhaps in the world, a more dissipated spot."

The world of genteel Natchez on the Bluffs and decadent Natchez Under the Hill could not coexist peacefully for long. As the civic leaders debated on

Probably the oldest brick home in Natchez, Texada was the meeting place for Mississippi's first state legislature.

courses of action, economic changes took care of their problem. The bandit-infested Natchez Trace fell into disuse as safer, more open roads were laid out. In 1812, Nicholas Roosevelt piloted the steamboat *New Orleans* up to a Natchez

Stephen Duncan entertained such illustrious guests as Henry Clay and Edward Everett Hale in the Greek Revival billiard hall on the lawn of Auburn.

wharf, opening the era of steam-powered river traffic and effectively putting the flatboaters and keelboaters out of business. Cotton was flowing out of Adams County fields and down to the wharves, and the men who would make money off that cotton had a vested interest in cleaning up the area. Natchez Under the Hill calmed down.

Less than twenty years after it was laid out, Natchez was entering its Golden Age. From 1810 to 1860, this was one of America's most prosperous corners. Cotton was the fuel of the economic engine, its profitability assured by Eli Whitney's cotton gin and Dr. Rush Nutt's superior Petit Gulf seed. Natchez had lost the title of territorial capital to nearby Washington in 1802, but it regained the honor when Mississippi became a state in 1817. Mayor Edward Turner was now living in Texada, and his home served as the first meeting place of the new legislature. Turner would go on to become Mississippi Attorney General, Speaker of the House of Representatives and Chief Justice of the state Supreme Court. It would have been convenient for him had the center of government remained on his doorstep, but political pressure statewide moved the capital to Jackson in 1822. Natchez was unfazed; its future was in cotton, not political rhetoric.

Riverboats were tying up at Natchez' wharves by the hundreds. As the cotton sailed off to New Orleans and Liverpool, the money poured into Natchez. In a tradition which would come to symbolize this city, large portions of that money began to be diverted into homebuilding. For fifty years, spanning the transition from the Federal style to the nation's finest examples of Greek Revival, Natchez would flaunt its wealth in a flurry of mansions.

Architect Levi Weeks had arrived in Natchez sometime before 1812, fleeing New England following a murder scandal. Weeks was versed in the classical traditions of architecture which were sweeping the northeastern U. S., and he designed a home for lawyer Lyman Harding which would incorporate those traditions into a breathtaking Federal mansion. Auburn was the first of Natchez' houses to be fronted with monumental columns, and it served as a model for many of the quintessential homes of the South which followed. Its massive brick solidity, decorated with finely carved frontispiece and semi-circular fanlight, was copied throughout the Federal period and into the Greek Revival era.

In 1820, Dr. Stephen Duncan acquired Auburn from Lyman Harding's estate. Duncan was a northerner with Natchez family connections who had moved to the area as a young medical school graduate in 1808. Two fortuitous marriages elevated him into the upper levels of Natchez society and possession of rich farmlands along the Homochitto River. He succeeded his uncle as president of the Bank of Mississippi, served in the Constitutional Convention of 1832 and was a founder of Trinity Episcopal Church.

Duncan was a slaveowner; as his agricultural interests prospered, he bought more land and more slaves until he was accurately regarded as the world's largest cotton planter and slaveholder. Six cotton plantations and two sugarcane estates were worked by over 1000 slaves, producing 4000 bales of cotton and 3000 hogsheads of sugar annually. Twenty-three house servants served the demands of Auburn, enlarged in 1827 with symmetrical wings. Such luminaries as Henry Clay and Edward Everett Hale were Duncan's guests in the mansion, joining him in the adjacent Greek Revival billiard hall for pool and bowling.

Auburn was built on the profits of the slave system. All the mansions of antebellum Natchez were; slavery was a fact of life which was considered inevitable, given the labor-intensive nature of cotton. Stephen Duncan owned more slaves than his neighbors, made more of a fortune from their efforts, and was more deeply troubled by the "Peculiar Institution." In 1831, he joined with several other Natchez aristocrats to form the Mississippi Colonization Society. Its purpose was to free and repatriate blacks to Africa. Duncan served as its president until 1840. Bucking public sentiment and increasing legal obstacles to manumission, he fought to turn the tide of enslavement.

Duncan's friend Isaac Ross died in 1836, leaving a will that stipulated his 175 slaves were to be freed and returned to Liberia. Duncan spent twelve years and a small fortune to implement Ross' wishes. Numerous court battles and parlor arguments dragged on while the slave population grew. Eventually, between 250 and 300 of Ross' slaves were sent to Liberia. Duncan personally smuggled seventy-five of them through the night to the Mississippi River banks to meet a New Orleans-bound boat.

One interested observer of Dr. Duncan's struggle was William Johnson, owner of Natchez' most successful barbershop. Politics and arguments swirled through his shop daily as the leaders of Natchez society were clipped and shaved. Johnson had three barbershops in all, adding to his income from a drayage service, a loan operation, a public bathhouse and a 750-acre plantation. He listened carefully to the raging debate over Stephen Duncan's organization, but he would never dare venture his opinion on the matter.

William Johnson was a "free man of color."

Johnson's father had been a white man, respected in Natchez circles, who freed Johnson's mother and sister when the boy was an infant. William was still technically a slave when Mississippi became a state; to free him, his father had to petition the legislature and receive a proclamation from Governor

Poindexter. Eleven-year-old William had his freedom and joined the small group of freedmen in Natchez. He was apprenticed to his brother-in-law, a successful barber, and by 1828 he was operating his own shop in Port Gibson. He returned to Natchez in 1830, bought out his brother-in-law, and started to look for other business opportunities.

Johnson hired free blacks to work in his barbershop, but he owned slaves to work in his secondary ventures. They hauled his whole-sale goods, ran a drayage wagon, chopped his cotton and collected outstanding loans. A white overseer, paid by Johnson, supervised the plantation. Despite his obvious business acumen and ambition, Johnson could not participate in politics or the leadership of Natchez. That town was home to almost half of Mississippi's free black population, and Johnson rose to the unofficial leadership of that select group.

Beginning in 1835, Johnson kept a secret diary, recording each day's news, scandals and observations gleaned in the barbershop. In 1841, he built a $2\frac{1}{2}$ story brick townhouse downtown, stuccoing the front and scoring it to resemble ashlar masonry. An elevated walkway connected the main house to a detached kitchen. Johnson and his wife raised ten children there.

The leader of a sizeable group of free blacks in antebellum Natchez built this home from the profits of his numerous ventures.

William Johnson was well-respected by the movers and shakers of Natchez. His status on the fringes of white society and obvious wealth stirred resentment among some of the town's less reputable figures. Baylor Winn owned land adjacent to Johnson's plantation, and they were constantly in dispute over boundaries. In 1851, Winn ambushed and murdered Johnson. His guilt was unequivocal, but his race was not. Winn was assumed to be a mulatto, but at trial he claimed to be white; that fact alone granted him immunity from prosecution for a black man's murder. Several juries failed to convict Winn and the murder went unavenged.

Johnson was eulogized at length in Natchez newspapers and buried in the Natchez Cemetery. The cruel system which had freed his murderer was dragging America toward dissolution. Stephen Duncan had assumed the presidency of the American Colonization Society in 1850, but soon after resigned in frustration. Like many of his neighbors in Natchez, even those who opposed his views on emancipation, Duncan was vehemently against secession. He saw Union dissolution as the death knell for Natchez and its way of life, and he began to contemplate returning to the North.

Dr. Haller Nutt was also a Unionist, but a more optimistic one than Stephen Duncan. Nutt was a planter, physician and scientist who had worked with his father, Dr. Rush Nutt, to develop improved cotton seeds. By 1840, the younger Nutt owned several plantations in Mississippi and Louisiana, including his plantation home at Winter Quarters, Louisiana. In 1850, he bought ninety acres of the old Longwood Plantation south of Natchez and began moving his family and headquarters there. His 800 slaves were divided between the Mississippi and Louisiana places. Many worked at Longwood, digging a lake and surrounding it with twenty acres of Julia Nutt's rosebushes. Five hundred varieties were in bloom, and she required a carriage to travel through the gardens.

By 1859, Haller Nutt was ready to tear down the original Longwood, move his family into a large brick servants' quarters and build his dream house. There was no shortage of models in Natchez to emulate. Brand new or still under construction were Greek Revival homes like Stanton Hall, Dunleith, Homewood and Magnolia Manor. The Federal mansions like Auburn, Rosalie and Arlington were aging gracefully. In the last days of antebellum Natchez, wealth and prominence were measured in the height of columns and the depth of verandas.

Nutt was not impressed with the Greek Revival and Federal showplaces of his neighbors. He had long admired the work of Philadelphia architect Samuel Sloan, whose work was frequently published in *Godey's Lady's Book*. Several of Sloan's ideas were based on the philosophy of Orson Squire Fowler, an eccentric phrenologist who promoted the advantages of octagonal structures. Nutt traveled to Pennsylvania to confer with Sloan and came away with plans for a house unlike any Natchez had ever seen.

When Sloan had drawn the sketches for "Design #49" in his *Model Architect of 1852,* he probably never expected to actually find anyone flamboyant enough to have it built. Six stories of brick, brackets, terraces and corbelled chimneys were topped with an enormous bulbous dome, looking for all the world like an overgrown Byzantine castle. This was exactly what Haller Nutt wanted, and Sloan must have thanked his lucky stars that Nutt's money and willingness to flaunt the architectural standards of Natchez had come his way.

Sloan made at least two trips to Natchez, walking the site with Nutt and seeing the project begun. With sectional tension building by the day, his future dealings with Nutt would be by mail. In March, 1860, Nutt wrote that he had sent fifteen men and eight boys to Longwood to begin burning bricks. They were slow and clumsy, turning out a product that would not be of the quality that was required. Sloan sent four master brick masons to facilitate the

For fifty years, spanning the transition from the Federal style to the nation's finest examples of Greek Revival, Natchez would flaunt its wealth in a flurry of mansions.

manufacture of 750,000 bricks. Within weeks, slaves were erecting the 27-inch thick walls on each of the 37-foot long façades. Brown's Sawmill under the bluffs was cranking out white and yellow pine boards for joists and rafters and cypress planks for the exterior woodwork. Gas lines and water pipes were sealed into the walls, rising one hundred feet from the basement to the upper floors.

Haller, Julia and the Nutt children were living comfortably in a brick building behind the construction. Eventually, it would be converted to a kitchen and servants' quarters. As the summer of 1860 gave way to fall, the family watched the house take shape. Climbing ladders into the dark recesses of the developing rooms, they could picture the nine bedrooms, ten-thousand volume library, school room, playrooms and formal areas. Crates arrived daily from New Orleans, filled with stonework and wood carvings rendered by master craftsmen in Pennsylvania. Orders went north for furniture and cabinetry to be made by George Hinkel, Philadelphia's foremost carpentry expert.

Dr. Nutt's dream was approaching reality when the fates turned against him. As the hammers and saws of skilled northern craftsmen echoed through the unfinished rooms and empty stair shafts of Longwood, a more ominous sound was heard in Charleston, South Carolina. The carpenters had grown increasingly uneasy as Mississippi seceded from the Union and war talk swirled through Natchez; when telegraph keys tapped out the news from Fort

Dr. Haller Nutt's octagonal masterpiece was never finished. Several generations of the family lived in the basement following the Civil War.

Sumter, the entire crew fled on the first boat going upriver. Their tools and aprons were left lying in the dust of the incomplete mansion.

Nutt was determined to finish the house. He wrote Sloan on May 19, 1861, advising him that the exterior of Longwood was almost complete. He would hire local workers and put his slaves to the task of finishing the rest. Four months later, only eight of twenty-six fireplaces had been finished, all in the basement. Another year passed, and still the cellar was the only livable space available. The Nutts reluctantly moved into those rooms and Haller ordered the doors and windows of the upper levels sealed against the elements.

In the earliest years of Natchez, the notorious "Natchez-Under-the-Hill" neighborhood was a hideout for robbers and ruffians. It has been refurbished and is now home to several shops and eateries.

The war which had dashed Nutt's plans reached Natchez in the spring of 1862. It was almost an anticlimax; the young men of the city had marched away a year before and left a ragtag group of old men and boys to defend the bluffs. The Silver Greys sullenly watched as the *USS Iroquois* dropped anchor in the Mississippi. Its commander sent a surrender demand to Mayor John Hunter, who mulled it over for twenty-four hours before bowing to the inevitable. Natchez surrendered without the first shot being fired and got on with the social season. Union gunboats returned in the fall; this time a trigger-happy Silver Grey fired at a ship, killing a seaman. The *USS Essex* began lobbing shells into Natchez and Natchez Under the Hill, killing seven-year-old Rosalie Beekman as she fled up Silver Street.

With the fall of Vicksburg in July, 1863, Natchez was placed under military occupation as a precaution. The Union presence was little more than a distraction to Haller Nutt. His plantation at Winter Quarters had been destroyed and his riches were gone. Wandering through the drafty hallways of his great shell of a house, he observed "I am ruined by this infernal secession." He had lost his land, his dream and his health. He died of pneumonia in June, 1864, at the age of 48. His widow blamed his death on the damp winds which whistled down from the empty dome of Longwood.

Julia Nutt was left with eight children and losses exceeding a million dollars. She petitioned the U. S. Government for reparations, reminding them that Dr. Nutt was a Unionist to the end. Eventually, she was awarded $200,000, but it was inadequate to complete Longwood. Julia lived on in "Nutt's Folly" for thirty-three years after Haller's death.

Longwood was never finished and Natchez was never the same. Even as cotton regained dominance as Mississippi's cash crop, Natchez was out of the loop. The loose soil of Adams County had eroded away, leaving deep gullies and worthless clay. The fifty years of phenomenal prosperity before the Civil War were memorialized forever in the mansions scattered around town, but their size and expense made them white elephants. Texada deteriorated and was threatened with demolition on a number of occasions. Natchez Under the Hill lost entire streets to the shifting waters of the Mississippi, and Silver Street dwindled to a handful of decrepit storefronts, all but forgotten when the Natchez-Vidalia Bridge opened and the last ferries stopped running. A box factory was built on the site of the ill-fated commandant's house at Fort Rosalie.

Stephen Duncan had left Natchez in disgust when the Civil War began. He died soon after the South surrendered, vindicated in his predictions of disaster. His family deeded Auburn and its vast lawns to the City of Natchez in 1911, designating it for use as a park.

William Johnson's descendants lived in his townhouse until 1938. Family lore preserved the memory of William's diary, and it was edited for publication in 1951. It remains in print, a remarkable mirror into the life of a free man in antebellum Natchez.

Texada was saved by Dr. and Mrs. George Moss in 1964. They lived in the carriage house for eight years while the old home was completely refurbished and restored. When the crumbling stucco was pulled away from Texada's façade, many of the bricks were found to be damaged. Master brickmasons carefully pulled out almost every brick, repointed them, and turned the inner side out towards the exterior.

Natchez Under the Hill was "rediscovered" by tourists wandering down Silver Street after touring the grand homes on the bluffs. Enterprising businessmen and restaraunteurs realized the potential for success in this unique sliver of Mississippi's history, and one by one the sagging buildings were refurbished and opened as eateries.

Longwood still sits empty but for its lavish basement. It passed through several generations of the Nutt family before being sold to the Pilgrimage Garden Club in 1968. In 1971, it earned the rare designation of National Historic Landmark. It will never be completed, and that finality adds to the emotional impact of the site. Longwood's legacy is not only as an architectural oddity, but in its symbolism of the end of the dream that was Natchez.

Vicksburg

Old Courthouse
Museum

his ball is at an end."

General Martin Luther Smith was hustling his officers out the door of Dr. William Balfour's home on Christmas Eve, 1862, having just received word of a flotilla of Union gunboats heading up the Mississippi River. His words signalled the end to holiday festivities, but they could also have been a statement on Vicksburg's fate. The largest and most prosperous town in Mississippi, considered an impregnable fortress on its high bluffs, was plunging into a nightmare of siege and surrender.

Vicksburg's site on the river had always attracted fortifications. French explorers built Fort St. Pierre here in the early 1700s but gave it little support; an Indian massacre wiped it out in 1729. Great Britain, Spain and the United States bickered over ownership after the American Revolution, but the area was so far from civilization that no one considered it prime property. The Spaniards built Fort Nogales in 1790. Their stay along the Mississippi was brief; most of the settlers in the surrounding village of Walnut Hills were American and British, and the Spanish lowered their flag and left in 1798. The Americans, citizens of the newly-created Mississippi Territory, renamed the small stockade Fort McHenry, but by 1800 it was all but unmanned. Walnut Hills struggled along as a distant outpost with a sprinkling of settlers.

Vicksburg's story really began when Newitt Vick immigrated to Mississippi from Virginia in 1806. He was a Methodist preacher and entrepreneur, eager to join his brothers Hartwell and Burwell in the rich lands of Jefferson County. Vick achieved some measure of success there and in 1812

Dedicated in 1909, the Mississippi Monument at Vicksburg National Military Park was the subject of bitter controversy in the state legislature.

Detail from the Mississippi Monument at Vicksburg National Military Park.

established a mission at Openwoods, a few miles inland from the river in Warren County. With an eye for business as well as heaven, he bought several hundred acres on the high bluffs overlooking the Mississippi. He would make his fortune, not from the meager contributions of his backwoods

Yazoo Diversion Channel as seen from the Vicksburg bluffs.

parishioners, but from the lots he would lay out as "Vicksburg." The first lot was sold in July, 1819; before Vick could even get the money into the bank, he was dead of yellow fever, along with his wife. Thirteen Vick children were orphaned.

Several of the Vick offspring were grown and married, and their families would populate the new town. John Lane took up the plans of his late father-in-law and actually laid out the streets and lots. Land sold quickly, and it was incorporated in January, 1825, as Vicksburg. The future looked bright; as soon as wharves could be built, steamboats and flatboats were tying up at the site. Cotton planters from near and far recognized the new port as the ideal place to ship their product down to New Orleans, and before long the dirt streets were filled with cotton wagons and merchants. Within ten years, the population had grown to 2,500, much larger than the struggling little capital city of Jackson fifty miles to the east and rivaling downriver Natchez. One of Mississippi's first railroads was completed from Vicksburg to Clinton in 1836, further securing the viability of the city.

The river brought instant prosperity to Vicksburg, but it also introduced some problems. Steamboats had evolved from mere cotton barges to floating pleasure palaces, and their passengers were easy prey for the gamblers and thieves who hung around the wharves. Saloons and gambling dens were going up as fast as private homes in Vicksburg. Respectable townspeople gave a wide berth to such unsavory establishments as the notorious

General Grant was roaming north Mississippi, trying to find a way to take Vicksburg and failing repeatedly. In the spring of 1862, a flotilla commanded by Admiral David Farragut ventured up the river from New Orleans, sending word to Vicksburg's defenses that surrender was expected. With their cannons perched several hundred feet above the enemy, the Confederates found this threat laughable. Intermittent bombardment of the city was ineffectual. Confederate generals P .G. T. Beauregard, Stephen D. Lee and Earl Van Dorn watched from the Courthouse tower as the ironclad *Arkansas,* barreling down from the Yazoo City Naval Yard, fought its way through the Union armada, causing considerable damage before exploding.

All was quiet until Christmas. Grant was stymied in north Mississippi by General Van Dorn's raid on Holly Springs, and the Confederate leaders felt secure enough to dress up and attend Dr. Balfour's Christmas Eve ball with their ladies. The night was well under way when a messenger burst in announcing the approach of Union gunboats from the north. Punch cups were discarded, apologies made and the Confederate leaders disappeared into the night to rally their troops. A skirmish at Chickasaw Bayou followed a few days later, but Vicksburg was still in no immediate danger.

After a disastrous foray into the backwaters of the Mississippi Delta, Grant moved his troops over to Louisiana and marched them through the swamps there. They were then ferried across the Mississippi River to Bruinsburg and fought their way through Port Gibson, Raymond, Jackson and Champion Hill in a matter of weeks. Now Vicksburg was in serious trouble. Confederate commander John C. Pemberton threw a ring of defenses nine miles long around the eastern edge of town and waited for reinforcements to come from General Joseph Johnston. They never arrived. Grant laid down twelve miles of lines facing the city and settled in for a siege.

For forty-seven miserable, muggy days, Vicksburg held its ground. Union and Confederate trenches were so close that soldiers talked with each other between skirmishes. As their safe little world crumbled around them, the people of Vicksburg retreated from their mansions and townhomes into hillside caves. Emma Balfour could not be long budged from her Crawford Street house; she cringed when the shells struck home and worried about her flower-pots out back. Her diary gives a vivid picture of the summer days of 1863:

> *We have spent the last two nights in a cave, but tonight I think we will stay at home. It is not safe I know, for the shells are falling all around us, but I hope none may strike us. Yesterday morning a piece of mortar shell struck the schoolroom roof, tore through the partition wall, shattered the door and then went into the door sill and down the side of the wall. Another piece struck in the same room and a third in the cement in front of the house. Such a large piece struck the kitchen also, but we see them explode all around us and as this is all the harm done to us yet, we consider ourselves fortunate.*

Not so fortunate were those huddled in caves, living on mule meat and melting in the stifling June heat. The soldiers' lot was even worse; thousands were wounded and carried into town to be cared for in private homes, churches or wherever room could be found. The Courthouse, a likely target for gunboat shelling, was strategically filled with Union prisoners. Two were released and rowed out to Admiral Porter's boat to inform him that a direct hit on the Courthouse would cause more Union casualties than Confederate. With the exception of a nicked portico corner, the Courthouse was spared serious damage.

Next door to Emma Balfour, General Pemberton was making his headquarters in the Willis House. The house was hit by shells at least twice, and Emma watched in horror as two horses were blown apart in the middle of Crawford Street. Gas lights burned in the Willis House late into the night; on

July 2, Pemberton summoned his brigade and division commanders to the mansion. He recalled the meeting years later: "Feeling assured that it was useless to hope longer for assistance from General Johnston, either to raise the siege of Vicksburg or rescue the garrison. . . . After much consideration, it was advised that I address a note to General Grant, proposing the appointment of commissioners to arrange terms of capitulation."

Pemberton's subordinates advised him that their exhausted troops were in no condition to survive a march of retreat out of the city; surrender was the only option. At 10:00 a.m. on the morning of July 4, Pemberton surrendered Vicksburg, with the agreement that his men could leave carrying their colors, unmolested. Emma Balfour described the sight of a defeated army streaming through the rubble of Vicksburg:

> *From twelve o'clock until late in the night the streets and roads were jammed with wagons, cannons, horses, men, mules, stock, sheep, everything you can imagine that appertains to an army. . . . Nothing like order prevailed, of course, as divisions, brigades and regiments were broken and separated. As the poor fellows passed, every house poured forth all it had to refresh them. I had every one on the lot and there were visitors carrying buckets of water to the corner for the men. Then on the back gallery I had everything that was eatable put out—and fed as many as I could.*

The scene at the Courthouse was different; jubilant Union soldiers paraded up the hill and watched as Lt. Colonel W. E. Strong and Sergeant B. F. Duggan of the Ohio Cavalry climbed the clock tower and replaced the Confederate flag with the Union colors. One soldier, stopping to notice the name "Baker Iron Company, Cincinnati, Ohio" stamped onto the iron stairway, mused at "the impudence of the people who thought they could whip the United States when they couldn't even make their own staircases."

Emma Balfour refused to leave her home for the safety of the caves during the Siege of Vicksburg. She described in vivid detail the horrors of war and her concern for such minor treasures as her flowerpots.

The Union flag may have been flying from the cupola of the Courthouse, but it would be a decade before Vicksburg truly rejoined the nation. Slowly, the debris from the shelling was cleared away and life resumed some degree of normalcy. St. Francis Xavier Catholic School, begun in the Cobb House across from Balfour House in late 1860, reopened its doors to students. The six nuns who had arrived from Baltimore in the last peaceful days before war had spent the conflict nursing the wounded and seeing their little school turned into a barracks, first for Confederates and then Union soldiers. The building was handed back to them in 1864, and they gratefully turned from medicine back to education. In 1868, Father Jean Baptiste Mouton designed an imposing Gothic Revival convent next door to the Cobb House, and over time the complex would grow to encompass the entire city block, with a huge auditorium, classroom buildings, a cow barn and cemetery.

A small group of Catholic nuns from the North endured the war years and remained to found St. Francis Xavier Catholic School. Their Gothic Revival convent was built in 1868.

A series of military and provisional governments controlled Vicksburg through the late 1860s and early 1870s. The economic engine of the city was humming soon after the war, as cotton crops again came in and the factories were back in business. Vicksburg even made a concerted effort to be declared capital of Mississippi in 1870, with its newspapers waging a vicious smear campaign against Jackson. The Warren County Courthouse was offered as a likely replacement for the decrepit Jackson statehouse and legislators were wined and dined on the river. To the disappointment of many, the effort was in vain.

By 1874, Vicksburgers had had enough of government by those they viewed as outsiders and crooks. The city and county were $1.4 million in debt. A Taxpayers League was formed with the purpose of placing the

The largest and most prosperous town in Mississippi, considered an impregnable fortress on its high bluffs, was plunged into a nightmare of siege and surrender.

Democratic Party back in power, and the elections of August, 1874, saw the league triumph. Tempers were still high, though, and, in December, five hundred league members marched on the Courthouse and forcibly removed the sheriff, coroner and circuit clerk. The sheriff fled to Jackson and appealed to Governor Adelbert Ames for help. Ames sent the sheriff back with a promise to back him with a militia company composed largely of freedmen. The two groups clashed, a riot ensued and dozens were killed and injured.

For a time, Vicksburg had two dueling governments. All over Mississippi, political change was in the air. By spring, 1876, Mississippi's Lieutenant Governor had been impeached and resigned, Governor Ames had left hastily under threat of the same and Mississippi was back in Democratic hands. Vicksburg could put the past fifteen years behind it and turn its attention back to the river which gave it life.

That river would deal the next blow to Vicksburg. Notoriously fickle, the Mississippi carries enough power to cut through land and reroute itself at will. It did just that in 1876, slicing into Louisiana and leaving Vicksburg high and dry. It would be twenty-eight years before a successful diversion canal brought the Yazoo River to Vicksburg's doorstep, but, fortunately, the economy was diverse enough to survive the abandonment by the Mississippi. Railroads had taken much of the traffic once carried on the river, and new lines were being built through the Delta and into Vicksburg.

Thousands of Union soldiers, many unknown, are buried in rows along the hillsides on the west side of Vicksburg National Military Park. All Confederate graves were moved elsewhere.

As the 1880s and 1890s turned toward the twentieth century, social life had returned to Vicksburg. The Courthouse hill had finally been terraced and Sunday afternoons found it filled with picnickers and bands. One of the favorite bands was sponsored by the B'nai Brith Literary and Social Club, an outgrowth of Vicksburg's large and prosperous Jewish community. Its purpose was "the intellectual and social advancement of its members" with those members "confined entirely to Israelites" by its constitution. The Ladies Society would make its first home in the old Balfour House, sold by that family in the late 1880s.

St. Francis Xavier Academy continued to grow and prosper, adding its vast auditorium in 1886. Within a few years, the sisters would also buy the Willis House (now known as Pemberton's Headquarters) and use it for decades as a boarding school and nursery school.

Mississippi was swept by Confederate nostalgia as the nineteenth century ended, with monuments and memorials popping up in every town. Naturally, this sentiment was magnified in Vicksburg, where the war had turned irreversibly into a losing cause. Colonel C. C. Floweree, the youngest Confederate officer to achieve that rank when it was conferred on him at age 20, was a veteran of Gettysburg who made a fortune in the postwar ice business. He organized a massive Blue-Gray reunion in Vicksburg in 1890, bringing in hundreds of aging veterans who could still pinpoint exactly where their trenches were dug and where each batallion was stationed. The momentum to establish a national park was underway, and in October, 1895, the Vicksburg National Park Association was formed. President William McKinley signed legislation in 1899 to formally authorize the park. Local landowners donated acreage to the cause, the largest grant being thirty acres from the Anshe Chesed Temple.

By 1900, nearly 2000 acres were under the control of the Park Association. Union and Confederate veterans walked the hills and valleys together, reliving those seven weeks which had changed American history. Markers were placed, landmarks noted and state legislatures across the country appropriated funds for memorials. Mississippi's legislature balked at paying for a monument; convoluted logic convinced the legislators that the Vicksburg Park, officially designated now as Federal land, was enemy territory once again. Park Commissioner Stephen D. Lee, his credibility bolstered by his own military record, finally won over enough lawmakers to pass the monument appropriation by one vote. A 76-foot-tall obelisk carved from Mount Airy granite was dedicated in 1909. Seated at its base is Clio, the Muse of History, inscribing the names of Mississippi's soldiers on her honor roll.

In 1905, the Yazoo River was successfully diverted into the Mississippi's old river bed, putting Vicksburg back in the riverboat business. Tourism was already a growing industry, capitalizing on the renewed interest in Civil War history. Visitors admired the antebellum mansions and the elaborate convent and auditorium of St. Francis Xavier. By 1915, the Academy lot was so crowded that the nuns moved their cows to the country and their cemetery to Cedar Hills. A few blocks away, the B'nai Brith Literary Club had built an elegant Italian Renaissance clubhouse to host its social activities. New Orleans architect Leon Weiss designed a semicircular porch with stone balustrades; the interior included a basement swimming pool, meeting rooms, a library and a third-floor ballroom complete with stage. The stage had the unique feature of opening both into the ballroom and onto the roof, offering indoor and outdoor entertainment. Weiss would go on to renown as the architect of the Louisiana Governor's Mansion and State Capitol.

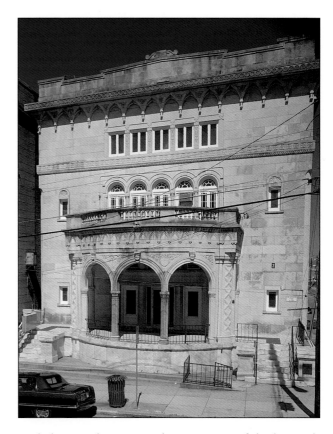

Vicksburg's vibrant Jewish community of the late 19th and early 20th century built the B'nai Brith Social Club as a social and literary gathering place. In later years, it served as the Vicksburg Police Department.

As in many other Mississippi cities, progress and prosperity brought hard choices for Vicksburg. Old houses were torn down for commercial development. Balfour House suffered through lean years when Emma's grand Christmas Ball was only a fading memory. It was used as a Masonic Hall, drug rehabilitation center, church and apartment house. By 1980, all of its fine exterior decorative elements were gone and it seemed doomed to demolition. A last-minute salvage effort restored it to its antebellum splendor, with Civil War-era photos guiding the changes. During the renovation, a large chunk of mortar shell fell from the upstairs ceiling, echoing the description of its path into the house written by Emma Balfour one hundred and seventeen years before. The house now matches its pre-war elegance, hosting a Christmas Ball each year where the interrupted party is reenacted.

Pemberton's Headquarters faded even more rapidly than Balfour House. After its days as a part of St. Francis Xavier's complex, it gradually deteriorated and was near collapse when renovation was finally begun.

As the twentieth century progressed, Vicksburg's Jewish community diminished, and the Anshe Chesed synagogue was torn down in 1982. The B'nai Brith Literary Society dwindled, and its building was sold to the city for use as a police department in the 1960s. The police have moved on to a more modern building, leaving the B'nai Brith Club empty and awaiting new purpose.

Even the venerable "Old Courthouse" was outmoded by 1939 and replaced with a more modern structure across the street. Demolition of the eighty-year-old building seemed logical to the Warren County supervisors, who wanted to free up this prime downtown lot for something more profitable. They were ready to forge ahead when they ran into an insurmountable obstacle by the name of Eva Davis. A lifelong Warren County resident with no political background, Eva took on the salvation of the Old Courthouse as her mission. She pestered and pleaded and wrote letters to anyone who would listen:

I do plead with you gentlemen not to make of this splendid edifice just another outmoded structure left to crumble to dust and be forgotten in the generations that march on. For cities are not remembered for their newness, but for their culture, their foresight and their history.

Eva spearheaded the formation of the Vicksburg and Warren County Historical Society. Attorneys in that group searched the title of Courthouse Hill and found that it was to have been Newitt Vick's chosen home site, deeded to the city by John Lane with the proviso that it be "For the use of public buildings so long as the public will occupy it . . . " Obviously, this hill was not going to be sold for commercial development. After years of Eva Davis' stubborn entreaties, the supervisors handed her a key and figured the intimidating task of salvaging the decrepit old building would hush her up.

They figured wrong. Faced with mountains of discarded papers and rubbish littering the hallways, years of dust and grime and an electrical system that was inadequate at best and downright dangerous at worst, Eva set to work. When she trudged up the steep steps from Cherry Street, hauling heavy buckets of water, the supervisors probably chuckled. When she made her umpteenth trip with those same buckets and cartloads of trash began to appear on the lawn, they realized that she was deadly serious about saving the Courthouse, singlehandedly if necessary. A few volunteers showed up to help

Eva Whitaker Davis almost singlehandedly saved the Old Courthouse from destruction. The museum, opened in 1948, has grown into one of the largest and most unusual collections of Mississippi memorabilia in the state.

with scrubbing and polishing, and Vicksburgers sorted through their attics for objects which would fill her museum. On June 3, 1948, Eva hoisted the American and Confederate flags to the top of the bell tower and the Old Courthouse Museum opened for its first visitors. In 1966, thousands of visitors later, the name was changed to "Old Courthouse Museum-Eva Whitaker Davis Memorial."

The Courthouse bell still tolls the hour, and it rings repeatedly on notable occasions. It rang in mourning for Eva Davis on the 1974 day when her funeral procession wound its way out of Vicksburg. Her legacy was secure, and the Old Courthouse would never again be threatened with loss by neglect. It towers over Vicksburg as a permanent monument to the city's fascinating history and the determination of a woman who would not let the past be forgotten.

Dominating the plan was the Capitol Green, a sweeping open space high above the backwaters of the Pearl.

Meeting in Columbia, the Legislature accepted Van Dorn's design, and the wheels began turning to convert this wilderness into a capital. In 1822, Mississippi's constitution was so simple and the government so blissfully limited that only a few buildings were deemed necessary for its purposes. A two-story brick statehouse was hastily constructed on the northeast corner of Capitol and President streets. The governor was advised to make his own arrangements for housing, and Jackson was open for business.

Unfortunately, nobody came. Proprietors of the expected hotels, taverns, livery stables and stores saw no reason to relocate to a village that only hosted a handful of legislators for a few weeks each year; the governor had such limited responsibilities that he saw no reason to come at all. Jackson's little statehouse sat empty for most of the year, surrounded by a few log huts and acres of mud that showed no promise whatsoever of developing into anything. Jackson's neighbor to the west, Mt. Salus, was growing by leaps and bounds. Boasting access to the Natchez Trace and a new college, this town which would become Clinton made a concerted push to claim the title of capital city. The Legislature, after several years of trekking to the depressing backwater on the Pearl, put the decision to a vote. Clinton lost by one vote; tempers flared, and duels were fought over this slight, but Jackson had secured a brief and tenuous hold on its status.

As the 1830s arrived, vast acreage was opening up for settlement after the Treaty of Dancing Rabbit Creek and Treaty of Pontotoc were signed. Before the Choctaws and Chickasaws could even begin their sad trek west to Oklahoma, their land was being snatched up for $1.25/acre, luring a surge of new settlers into Mississippi. Senator Robert J. Walker summed up the feeling of those awed by the tripling of the state's population: "Kentucky's coming, Tennessee's coming, Alabama's coming, and they're coming to join the joyous crowds of Mississippians." America had a new land of dreams, and it was called Mississippi.

A state on the move needed a new constitution, and the one put together in 1832 vastly complicated and expanded the role of government and the duties of the governor. A shabby little cluster of government buildings in a town that couldn't attract citizens was not going to get the job done. Communities with more to offer were lobbying for the prestige which capital designation would bring. But the legislature was committed to this central location and resolved to give Jackson an eighteen-year reprieve. The capital would remain there until 1850; if Jackson didn't live up to its promise, the honor would be awarded to the highest bidder.

Jackson's few civic boosters, energized by their close brush with oblivion, decided that they had best get to work on earning their place in Mississippi's future. A proposal was made to sell off several of the empty, undeveloped public squares from Peter Van Dorn's original plans, with the proceeds earmarked for a more suitable statehouse. The 1832 Constitution also mandated that the governor must establish residence in Jackson, and Jacksonians began to lobby the legislature for funds to build a "suitable house" for the chief executive. Realizing that the handful of people who called Jackson home could not develop a capital city without help, the legislature appropriated $95,000 for the new statehouse and $10,000 for the Governor's Mansion.

Finally, the future of Jackson began to brighten. Progress was still slow and occasionally laughable. Professional architects

The design for the capitol was monumental, keeping with Mississippi's position as one of the fastest-growing and most prosperous states in the Union.

*A*merica had a new land of dreams, and it was called Mississippi.

and builders were a scarce commodity on the frontier. Governor Abram Scott hired the first applicant for state architect, John Lawrence, apparently overlooking Lawrence's spelling of his profession as "architeck." With great ceremony, the cornerstone of the new capitol building was laid in 1834 on the Capitol Green. As the Gothic structure took shape, work was halted by financial problems; when it resumed, even the untrained eyes of Jackson's sidewalk supervisors could discern that whatever this pile was that Lawrence was building, it was going to be a disaster. Governor Hiram Runnels finally took matters in hand and fired the inept Lawrence, turning instead to William Nichols. A native of Bath, England, Nichols had served as state architect for North Carolina, and his mastery of the emerging Greek Revival style would leave an architectural legacy in Mississippi which still shines in the Old Capitol, Governor's Mansion and Lyceum Building in Oxford.

Nichols valiantly attempted to salvage the mess that Lawrence had created on the Capitol Green, but found it totally unacceptable. The walls were knocked down and building began from scratch. Assigned the quadruple duty of constructing a statehouse, penitentiary, governor's mansion and insane asylum, Nichols chose to concentrate on first putting a roof over the heads of the legislators and criminals, leaving the mentally defective and governor on their own for a few more years.

Nichols' design for the capitol was monumental, in keeping with Greek Revival styles and Mississippi's position as one of the fastest-growing and

The Governor's Mansion was designed by William Nichols, who also built the Old Capitol and the Lyceum at Ole Miss. It narrowly escaped the widespread destruction which left Jackson a "Chimneyville" during the Civil War.

In six years' time, Jackson was transformed from a muddy embarrassment into a sparkling capital city, anchored by classical buildings to rival any in America.

most prosperous states in the Union. The main floor was of stone quarried in nearby Utica; the upper floors were brick burned on the grounds, covered with stucco and scored to resemble stone. Six massive Ionic columns rose above stone arches to support a huge pediment. Capping the roof was a windowed dome, visible for miles across the countryside. Inside, twin stairs curved from the ground floor into the upper stories, and the central rotunda soared from the main level into the tip of the dome. The legislative chambers, each accentuated by classic columns, were housed in the north and south wings of the building. The very enormity of this impressive capitol must have been breathtaking to Jacksonians, towering over the rude buildings which had sprung up in the brief years of the city's existence.

A few blocks to the northwest, Nichols was also overseeing construction of the state penitentiary. Its castle-like walls and parapets were stark and forbidding, surely a deterrent to Mississippi's criminal element. The Financial Panic of 1837 curtailed work on both the capitol and the penitentiary for several months, but the statehouse was ready for use by 1839 and the jail soon afterwards. The cost of the capitol had ballooned to $400,000, but Mississippians had a building to rival that of any state.

William Nichols now turned his attention to that "suitable house" for the governor; for almost twenty years, Mississippi's highest elected officials had been forced to find lodging in whatever flea trap or boarding house might be available, leaving their families at home. One of Van Dorn's green spaces, just a few blocks west of the capitol, was designated an appropriate site, and work began in earnest in late 1839. Once again, Nichols demonstrated his mastery of the Greek Revival form; he designed a simple two-story block of a building rendered exceptional by its classical details and impressive portico. Nichols' stated intention was to ". . . avoid a profusion of ornament, and to adhere to a plain republican simplicity, as best comporting with the dignity of the State." He accomplished just that, embellishing a symmetrical façade with a curving portico and four ornate Corinthian columns.

Funds for the mansion ran out in 1840 and work was halted without the roof line being adequately sealed, leading to leakage and interior wall damage which would plague governors for one hundred and fifty years. When construction resumed in 1841, Nichols was under tremendous pressure to complete the house for the inauguration of Tilghman Tucker. He failed, but six rooms of the rear family quarters were completed soon after Tucker's 1841 inauguration, and the governor's family moved in. The first of countless controversies to swirl about the mansion was not long in coming. State Treasurer Richard Graves accused Nichols of misappropriating funds in the building of the mansion. A legislative investigation revealed that Graves, not Nichols, was responsible for the shortfall in funds, and Graves was arrested. Allowed a brief visit with his wife, Graves appropriated her clothes and strolled out of the jail in disguise, fleeing the state. History doesn't reveal the fate of his wife.

In six years' time, William Nichols had transformed Jackson from a muddy embarrassment into a sparkling capital city, anchored by classical buildings to rival any in America. Jacksonians could breathe a bit easier, the threat of abandonment in 1850 diminishing with every new business and factory. Nationally prominent visitors such as Andrew Jackson, Henry Clay and Mexican War hero Jefferson Davis made their way to the city for appearances, where once they would have stopped only in Natchez and perhaps Vicksburg. Mississippi was growing both economically and demographically, its cotton fields supplying vast riches for many and its political power in Washington expanding.

The dawn of the 1850s found Mississippi leading the South in cotton production and overnight fortunes. Life was grand if you were a Natchez planter or a prosperous Holly Springs merchant, not so grand if you were a slave doomed to a lifetime of backbreaking labor. Sectional tensions were increasing as the issues of slavery, states' rights and secession came to a head. Predictably, the first serious saber-rattling in Mississippi emanated from the Governor's Mansion. John Anthony Quitman was inaugurated in January, 1850, and by the end of that year, he had called the legislature into special session to consider separation from the Union. Quitman was soon forced from office over unrelated misdeeds and cooler heads prevailed, but the die was cast. Over the next ten years, just as the state and Jackson were enjoying unparalleled prosperity and promise, Mississippi would be marching inexorably down the path of disaster.

In 1860, John J. Pettus moved his family into the mansion on Capitol Street. He was a fire-breathing secessionist, dedicated to following South Carolina out of the Union as soon as a war could be provoked. Despite strong Unionist sentiment in the old river counties and the Delta, the Ordinance of Secession was passed in the capitol in January, 1861. Thousands gathered on the Capitol Green, awaiting the proclamation and celebrating along Capitol Street when secession was declared from the statehouse's wrought-iron balcony. Mississippi was plunging headlong into a conflict which would decimate it economically, politically and socially, destroying most of a generation of her young men in the process. War would not reach Jackson for more than two years. But by the time William Tecumseh Sherman

City limits would be pushed out three times as the population tripled in only ten years. Jackson was on the verge of becoming a truly cosmopolitan southern community.

and Ulysses S. Grant fought their way into the capital city, all patience with Confederate resistance was long gone and complete and total destruction was the order of the day.

Jackson's strategic importance in the Civil War lay in its railroad lines and its ability to supply the much more valuable Vicksburg with munitions and necessities. After months of futile strikes at Vicksburg by water and land, General Grant marched thousands of troops through the swampy Louisiana Delta and ferried them across to Bruinsburg, south of Port Gibson. Confederate forces were driven back at Port Gibson and Raymond, and Jackson found itself, in May of 1863, in an uncomfortable predicament. Sherman was instructed to destroy all railroad links to Vicksburg and any munition factories which might still be supplying Southern troops. Confederate generals John C. Pemberton and Joseph Johnston huddled with Governor Pettus in the mansion, planning battle strategy and evacuation scenarios.

As Sherman's troops ravaged the countryside, Pettus ordered the government out of Jackson, beginning an odyssey that would find the capital moved from Meridian to Macon to Columbus, back to Macon and essentially into limbo. General Johnston rode into Jackson on May 13th and found it an eerily deserted ghost-town, the mansion standing open and no life in the streets. He torched the railroad depot and its supply buildings, blew up bridges over the Pearl River and left the remains of the city to Sherman's dis-

the corner in front of the Capitol heading north, they were rolling onto a North State Street which was soon to become a symbol of post-war wealth and social standing. From the Capitol to Fortification Street, the streetcar passed new mansions with white columns and the exuberant towers and turrets of Victorian architecture. Jackson was attracting a new breed of businessmen and philanthropists, eager to put the horrors of war and sectional strife behind them and lead the state into the last years of the century.

One of the most influential and successful North State Street nabobs was Reuben Webster Millsaps, a Copiah County native who earned a distinguished record in the Civil War and then lost no time in making a fortune trading cotton and running a wholesale business in St. Louis. In the 1880s, he purchased two prime lots on North State, just a few blocks north of the capitol, and built an impressive two-story Queen Anne mansion with corner towers and intersecting roof lines. Contrasting paint emphasized the geometric irregularity of the design, and its location on a hill accentuated its height. Major Millsaps was active in the development of several Jackson banks, as well as being heavily involved personally and financially in local causes. Believing strongly that the local young men should not have to venture even so far as Oxford to receive an education, he became the dominant force behind the founding of the college which would be named for him. His adopted daughter, Josie, would marry the son of Lewis Fitzhugh, another Jackson philanthropist who founded Belhaven College for Jackson's young women. "Suburbs" would grow up around these colleges as Jackson broke free of its original boundaries. Lining both sides of North State Street leading to those suburbs would be a profu-

Major Reuben Webster Millsaps chose the highest lot on North State Street for his 1880s Queen Anne mansion. He would provide the financial impetus for the founding of Millsaps College in 1890.

The Millsaps-Buie House escaped the fate of so many of its North State Street neighbors, withstanding the rush to commercialization which decimated the once-proud residential stretch.

sion of mansions, an architectural display of wealth and power which was rivaled only by the antebellum townhouses of Natchez.

In 1890, Mississippi's legislative leaders wrote a new constitution for the state, one which would be creaking along in a much-altered form more than one hundred years later. As the old century wound down and the new one approached, Jackson was on the verge of explosive growth. Technology was changing everything about people's lives. The trolley mules had been retired and miles of new electric streetcars replaced them, taking townspeople to the far stretches of their growing city. The population would triple in ten years and the city limits would have to be pushed out three times in that same period. Jackson was on the verge of becoming a truly cosmopolitan southern community.

In its headlong rush to the next century, Jackson was in danger of leaving its soul behind. Its proud antebellum prizes, the capitol and the Governor's Mansion, were crumbling. Construction mistakes made during the 1830s, the effects of war and a perpetual refusal by the legislature to fund the most basic maintenance had taken their toll. Lawmakers feared for their very lives in the capitol; this "pitiful object of neglect" was sagging visibly, its exterior walls pulling away from each other and its interior plaster raining down on the heads of wary visitors. Adding to the wear and tear of age was a clutter problem. For years, every unwanted book and scrap of paper generated by the government had been relegated to the old library on the third floor. As the weight of these tomes increased, the joists supporting the entire room began to sag, leading lawmakers to consciously avoid the room beneath it. Greek Revival was "old-fashioned;" legislators wanted a new building and were more than willing to fund the demolition of this dangerous fossil.

After a decade of arguing and dodging falling plaster, the legislature and governor finally reached a decision. The fortress-like penitentiary, rebuilt

In its headlong rush to the next century, Jackson was in danger of leaving its soul behind. Its proud antebellum prizes were crumbling.

after the Civil War, was increasingly an embarrassment to well-heeled Jacksonians. The vast empty spaces of the Delta seemed a much more appropriate locale to house prisoners; the jail would be torn down and its ten-acre site dedicated to a new capitol. Funding, as always, was a stumbling block. When the state Supreme Court decided in Mississippi's favor in a million dollar suit with the railroads, the money was quickly steered toward the building project. Governor Andrew Longino toured other state capitols and Washington, D.C., observing architectural trends and popular styles. There being no state architect with the credentials of a William Nichols, a contest was held and fourteen designs were submitted. The winner was Theodore Link of St. Louis. He proposed a white Beaux Arts façade, reminiscent of the national capitol, which would dominate the new site just as the original statehouse had done at the top of Capitol Street.

Demolition began on the old penitentiary; long-standing legend maintains that some of its walls were so solidly planted in the Jackson dirt that they could not be removed, and perhaps they exist under some of the rather odd mounds of landscaping on the New Capitol grounds. Construction of the new building began with the first shovelfuls of dirt on January 1, 1901. Apparently trying to stay in the good graces of the Supreme Court, the Illinois Central Railroad ran a special spur line to the site, facilitating the process of building and helping to bring the project in under budget and in record time.

Mississippi had a shiny new house of government for the people to

Incorporating portions of Jackson's first two public schools, Central High has undergone several renovations and briefly served as the State Capitol after its educational mission was finished.

admire and for legislators to while away their hours in, but what was to be done with its predecessor, now referred to (with some derision) as the "Old" Capitol? When the legislature and state offices moved across downtown in 1903, it was left empty and dangerously unstable. Crowds flocking through the State Street entrance gates to the State Fair gave it a wide berth; those brave or foolhardy enough to enter found the ceiling of the Senate collapsed onto moldy carpets and paint hanging off the walls in sheets.

One of the last state officials to vacate the Old Capitol for the New Capitol was the head of the newly-created Department of Archives and History, Dunbar Rowland. Devastated by the possibility of losing this most tangible and dramatic of all Mississippi's historic sites, Rowland and his wife, Eron, campaigned ceaselessly for thirteen years for its renovation. Rallying various state patriotic groups to the cause, they finally convinced the legislature to appropriate money to shore up the retired statehouse. New Capitol architect Theodore Link supervised the complete excavation of the building's interior, ripping out all of the leaning walls and replacing them with a steel skeleton which would last until major renovations were done in the late 1950s. The Old Capitol would find new life as a state office building and its next threat would be blocked by yet another Archives and History stalwart, Charlotte Capers.

The Old Capitol wasn't the only Jackson landmark on the brink of extinction as the nineteenth century rolled over into the twentieth. Governor Longino, who had pushed long and hard for the New Capitol, saw no hope for his own home. The Governor's Mansion was also a victim of benign neglect and legislative indifference. Downtown Jackson was enjoying a real estate boom, and more than one businessman was eyeing the prime block of Capitol Street property occupied by the decaying mansion and its ragtag assortment of outbuildings. In 1902, Capitol Street was widened, bringing down oaks planted by Governor Foote's wife in 1852; it seemed as if Jackson would just close in on this worn-out reminder of a simpler time.

By 1904, outgoing Governor Longino was begging the legislature for emergency repairs just to maintain a safe living environment in the mansion. His successor, James K. Vardaman, addressed the crowds at his inauguration with a suggestion to either sell or tear down this "relic of aristocracy." He was not happy with his appointed accommodations, but still moved his family into the house and left his cow to graze in the back yard. Four years of occupancy changed his mind about the value of the mansion. Mrs. Vardaman planted a magnolia at the southwest corner of the grounds in honor of James K. Vardaman, Jr.'s twelfth birthday. Vardaman himself was known to carve initials into the trees of the grounds, and by the time his farewell speech to the legislature rolled around, he was pleading for the preservation of the mansion. Calling it a "monument to the best in the state's history . . . the only landmark left to testify of the good old days of long ago," he urged those controlling the state coffers to pour some money into it posthaste.

If Vardaman spoke eloquently with his words, incoming Governor Edmond Noel spoke even more effectively with his feet. Judging his family's safety to be more important than protocol, Noel moved his clan into a Jackson hotel. The *Clarion-Ledger,* traditionally opposed to any state expendi-

Jackson's first public high school for Black students was the dream of Alderman Smith Robertson. The building now houses an African-American cultural center and museum which bears his name and details the struggle for equality in the state.

tures on moldy antiques of bygone days, took this as a golden opportunity to get rid of an eyesore. Editors railed against this "dangerous old hulk, a menace to life and property," which should disappear as quickly as possible.

The newspaper's intention was to spur public sentiment toward demolition. Instead, what it managed to stir up was a hornet's nest of protest among Mississippi's women. The United Daughters of the Confederacy, the Daughters of 1812, even the Women's Christian Temperance Union and the Old Ladies Home Association, joined by the United Confederate Veterans, descended in droves on the legislature and began a letter-writing campaign to state newspapers filled with righteous indignation. These were the same indomitable ladies who had planted Confederate monuments and memorials on every courthouse square around the state, and they were not to be trifled with when it came to matters of Mississippi history. Governor Noel moved his bags back down the street, invited the legislators in to see just how bad things were, and happily walked away from the New Capitol with a $30,000 repair appropriation. The formal front rooms were restored, the grand stair relocated, the old family annex torn down and replaced with a modern two-story apartment, and the ramshackle collection of outbuildings demolished. The Governor's Mansion had joined the Old Capitol in that "untouchable" category of Mississippi's historic architecture.

While preservation wars raged downtown, Jackson was bursting at the seams, growing northward toward Asylum Heights and westward toward the old Livingston Plantation. Downtown was being transformed. Capitol Street was bustling daily with Model Ts and electric trolleys; Farish Street boasted an entire business district frequented and owned by blacks. Jackson's future leaders had to be educated in style, and Central High was expanded and remodeled around the core of the city's first two public school buildings. Just a few blocks away, Smith Robertson School was built in 1909. Its very existence was in large part due to the courageous battle of its namesake, a Jackson barber who managed to hang on to his seat as an alderman and pushed tirelessly for black education through the early years of Jim Crow segregation. A few years before it was expanded with an ornate Art Deco façade, Smith Robertson would salute Richard Wright as its 1925 valedictorian. He accepted his diploma and headed off to literary fame in the same year that Central High sent Eudora Welty into the world of words.

Governors in the newly renovated mansion could sit in their front parlor and watch progress on the first of Jackson's "skyscrapers." The architects for the Lamar Life Building were instructed to blend their design with the Gothic ecclesiastical beauty of St. Andrew's Cathedral. They responded with a thirteen-story gray brick edifice, complete with clock tower, parapets and hovering gargoyles. The Seth Thomas clock faces would come to be as much a Jackson landmark as the Old Capitol's dome and the New Capitol's eagle.

Jackson had finally come of age. From the inauspicious beginnings of Lefleur's Bluff, through repeated attempts by sister cities to usurp the role of government, even war and Reconstruction, the city had prevailed and established its rightful place among America's capitals. Its historic structures would be altered and rebuilt, but never again seriously threatened by the march of progress. The Old Capitol was completely reconstructed in the late 1950s, finding a permanent home as the State Historical Museum; the Governor's Mansion underwent extensive refurbishment and replacement of the family annex in the 1970s. Neither Central High nor Smith Robertson School survived the upheaval of desegregation with their educational mission intact. Central High was converted to state offices and even served as a quasi-Capitol while that building underwent renovation, and Smith Robertson is the site of an African-American cultural center detailing the struggle for equality in Mississippi. The Millsaps-Buie House escaped the fate of so many of its

State Street's original skyscraper was designed to be visually compatible with its neighbor, St. Andrew's Episcopal Church. Its gargoyles have loomed over the Governor's Mansion since the 1920s.

North State Street neighbors, withstanding the rush to commercialization which decimated that once-proud residential stretch.

The Capitol eagle is nearing its century mark, coming down only once for a fresh coat of gold leaf and then rising again to its high perch above the city. It now looks out over a city that has learned to value the brick and mortar of its youth, preserving them for future generations.

Columbus

Callaway Hall

$\mathcal{I}$f the Mississippi River was the magnet for early settlement in western Mississippi, the Tombigbee was its counterpart in the east. Along the Tombigbee, the site that the Indians called Pleasant Ridge was a perfect spot for a town, located high on a bluff above the river's east bank. Some semblance of a fort was built there before 1800, and a small village grew up nearby.

Treaties in 1816 with the Choctaw and Chickasaw Indians opened the lands east of the Tombigbee while Mississippi was still a vast empty territory. As the population grew, roads were laid out to take advantage of the river. Gaines Trace was an important route running from Monroe County's Cotton Gin Port down to Pleasant Ridge. Andrew Jackson built a Military Road from Tennessee to New Orleans; Pleasant Ridge was his chosen ferry site across the Tombigbee. Gaines Trace and the Military Road crossed on Pleasant Ridge. Traffic quickly built up on those two highways and it was evident that some sort of a town would develop on the bluffs. With all the beauty of nature to attract settlers, it deserved a name reflecting the attributes of the area. What it got was "Possum Town."

Thomas Moore built his log cabin a few hundred feet east of the bluffs and waited for neighbors. One of the first to arrive was Spirus Roach. Roach must have been a man of extraordinary homeliness; the local Indians found his resemblance to the lowly possum entertaining and dubbed the little village "Possum Town." Unfortunately, the name stuck.

Despite its less-than-grand designation, Possum Town was obviously going to make it as a townsite. Dr. Gordon Lincecum was an early arrival

Major Thomas G. Blewett filled the extensive grounds of his estate with formal gardens and fanciful iron animals. Several of these animals survived the fire which destroyed Columbus High School and endangered the mansion.

One of many architecturally outstanding antebellum mansions in Columbus, the Blewett-Harrison-Lee house was home to General Stephen D. Lee and later a part of Columbus High School.

from Tuscaloosa, Alabama and recorded his first impression of the site:

I found it a beautifully elevated situation . . . an eligible town site . . . it would be a town as soon as the country should settle up . . . I went home, sawed a thousand boards, put them on a raft and floated them down the river, with the intention of building a snug little house on a nice place.

By 1821, the legislature had taken notice of the growing community in the far reaches of Mississippi, and a commission was dispatched to survey the site and lay out a plat. When it came time to incorporate in 1822, businessman Silas McBee stepped forward with a suggestion which would save future generations the embarrassment of being known as "Possum Towners." McBee suggested the more formal "Columbus," which was quickly accepted. The surveyors laid out a grid plan with large square blocks of ten lots each. William Moore was elected the first mayor, and Columbus was on its way to becoming one of antebellum Mississippi's largest and most successful cities.

In a common thread which repeatedly weaves itself through the history of Mississippi towns, education was as vital an issue to early settlers as food and shelter. Columbus was no exception. By coincidence, Columbus was laid out on sixteenth section land, with all property leased by the state and the proceeds dedicated to education. Dr. Lincecum's guidance steered those funds into the creation of Franklin Academy, the state's first free public school. It was a small start, just a 30'x 40' frame building, but it preceded any other free school in Mississippi by twenty-four years.

Columbus grew rapidly through the 1820s, boosted by steamboat traffic on the Tombigbee and the continued development of the agricultural regions east of town. By 1830, over 3,000 people were living in the area, justifying the creation of Lowndes County from the southern part of Monroe County. The last two Mississippi Indian treaties in 1830 and 1832 opened up vast

For the next three decades, this area would see remarkable riches made and a high degree of culture achieved.

acreage west of the Tombigbee for development, and Columbus found itself with the busiest land grant office in America. For the next three decades, this area would see remarkable riches made and a high degree of culture achieved. The population of Lowndes County quadrupled between 1830 and 1840, and elegant public buildings and private homes appeared all over Columbus. The first courthouse was built in 1832; in 1835, Franklin Academy's little building was replaced by two large brick schoolhouses, one for boys and one for girls.

The most enduring architectural achievement in antebellum Columbus was its homes. The first houses on the bluffs were crude log huts. As fortunes were made in the fertile prairie lands along the river, planters established a tradition of building town houses rather than plantation manors. Often, they would purchase an entire city block and fill it with a mansion, servants' quarters, smokehouses and garden structures. Greek Revival style predominated, with its square-paneled columns, transomed doorways and rooftop cupolas or belvederes. Interiors were equally grand, filled with curving grand staircases, marble mantels and elaborately carved ceiling medallions and molding. Some builders favored Italianate or Gothic elements; five houses were built in a "Columbus Eclectic" style which combined Italianate, Gothic and Greek Revival features in a unique fashion.

James S. Lull was the architect responsible for many of Columbus' most notable buildings, both public and private. He arrived from Vermont in 1837 and would spend the next thirty years carving an indelible niche in the histo-

Anyone who could hold a hammer or draw a house plan found work among the myriad mansions and storefronts which were rising all over town.

ry of Mississippi architecture. In 1847 alone, Lull was involved in at least three projects which would have a lasting impact on the Columbus streetscape. Lowndes County's original courthouse was woefully inadequate for such a fast-growing city, and Lull was hired to design a new one. The cornerstone was laid in July, 1847, and when finished it was a monumental building with engaged brick pilasters and molded brick capitals. A two-story square tower rose from the middle of the roof, its round dome visible across the Tombigbee River.

A few blocks east of the new courthouse, Lull was also overseeing construction of a town house for Major Thomas G. Blewett. Blewett was a wealthy landowner who had migrated to Columbus in 1835 from South Carolina. A philanthropist as well as a successful planter, his cotton fortunes financed a bridge over the Luxapalilla River and the building fund of the Baptist Church. Now he would follow the tradition of his neighbors and build a fine house on several downtown acres. He bought all of Square 17 except for the two corner lots occupied by the Masonic Lodge and St. Paul's Episcopal Church. As Blewett's two-story brick house rose and overshadowed the modest church, the rector noted sadly that "Our church looks like a little ornamental gardener's lodge. . . ." Blewett may have had designs on making it just that. The south end of his home was a large conservatory overlooking formal English gardens. Life-size cast iron animals were scattered throughout the gardens.

James Lull in 1860. In 1884, when the Industrial Institute and College formally opened, Mississippi could claim the honor of having the first state-supported college for women in the nation.

The dawn of the twentieth-century found a prosperous Columbus heading into a period of rapid growth. R. H. Hunt of Chattanooga was the favored architect for public buildings; in 1901, he completely redesigned Lull's 1847 courthouse, converting it into a Beaux Arts style while retaining the clock tower. Downtown Columbus filled with impressive businesses and offices, losing all trace of its log-cabin origins.

In 1915, the Blewett-Harrison-Lee House had passed to yet another generation. General Lee's son was a lawyer for the Illinois Central Railroad, living in Chicago, and he didn't need an antebellum mansion in Mississippi. The house was given to the city with the stipulation that it must be used for educational purposes. Columbus High School was built on the site of the old gardens; the home's conservatory wing was removed and the house was actually attached to the school to serve as its home economics department. Generations of Columbus girls learned to cook in the refurbished kitchen and to set the table in the huge formal dining room. Columbus High burned in 1959, mercifully sparing the house. Under the direction of the Columbus Historical Society, it was turned into a museum. Major Blewett's iron animals still stand guard in the front yard of the Blewett-Harrison-Lee House.

St. Paul's remains on its 1854 site, its facade unchanged over a century-and-a-half. For most of those years, a Victorian rectory occupied the adjoining lot. When Walter Dakin served as St. Paul's rector in the first years of the twentieth century, his daughter and grandson, Thomas Lanier Williams, shared the home with him. Thomas would leave Columbus as a child, but as playwright "Tennessee" Williams, he recalled fond memories of his earliest years in the shadow of St. Paul's.

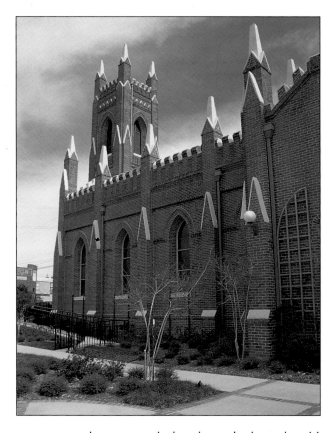

St. Paul's Episcopal Church was built on the old circus grounds and was barely finished before the onset of the Civil War. It would later be the playground for young Tennessee Williams, whose grandfather served the church as rector.

The original Industrial Institute building was home to thousands of girls at Mississippi State College for Women before it was declared a hazard and closed in the early 1930s. Renovated in 1938, Lull's masterpiece was renamed Callaway Hall in honor of Mary J. S. Callaway, mistress of mathematics and twice acting president of the "W." A complete gutting and remodeling in the 1960s brought it up to modern standards and it still dominates the entrance to Mississippi University for Women.

Friendship Cemetery, Columbus's burial ground for one hundred and fifty years, now holds over nine thousand graves. Many of the markers are elaborate and expensive, including a miniature Gothic mausoleum. None speak more eloquently of human sacrifice and forgiveness than the two thousand Confederate markers in long rows, shaded by magnolias planted soon after the war. A faded record book uncovered in the caretaker's attic in 1976 gave names to 298 soldiers and one Confederate army nurse, adding their identities to 47 others with engraved marble markers. In an ironic twist of fate, they are joined at Friendship by General S. D. Lee, the man who may have ordered the first fatal shots of the Civil War; not far away are buried the ladies of Decoration Day, who ended that war in the minds and hearts of America with their unselfish devotion to duty.

Holly Springs

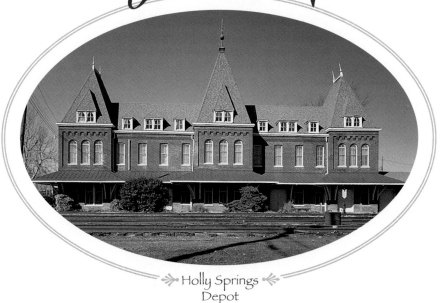

Holly Springs
Depot

This was the fourth building erected by the Presbyterians of Holly Springs, with construction beginning in 1858. It was incomplete when Union troops commandeered it for a stable and ammunition depot in 1862. Bored soldiers took target practice on the bricks and pews.

$\mathcal{N}$ot many trains stop at the Holly Springs Depot any more. When they do, it's just to tighten a shaky wheel or uncouple an empty boxcar. There hasn't been a passenger train through here in years, and the mule-drawn trolley which once rumbled from the tracks to Courthouse Square went to the scrap heap decades ago.

Once, every whistle-stop village in Mississippi boasted a depot, some utilitarian and others a bit more fanciful. But the grandest by any standard was the Holly Springs Depot. Much more than a loading dock or a traveling salesman's refuge, this station with its built-in hotel was a destination in itself. Its triple towers could be seen for hundreds of yards up the tracks, and when travellers stepped off the train here they were greeted with the sounds of a Memphis dance band playing in the ballroom and the smell of French cooking wafting from the kitchen.

The Depot that stands today was built in 1886, during a resurgent period for Holly Springs. In its fifty-year history to that point, this town had mushroomed from nothing, swung from economic highs to financial ruin, survived war and political turmoil and lost a significant part of its population in a tragic epidemic. The Depot was a symbol of its resiliency, a high-water mark before changing times and trends left it behind.

Of all the towns which sprang up practically overnight in 1830s Mississippi, Holly Springs was the closest to being an instant success. Chickasaw tribal leaders signed away their ancestral lands in 1832; before their people could even gather together their few material possessions for the long

Clear springs bubbling out of a holly grove were a prime discovery, quickly drawing enough newcomers to warrant the formation of a town.

trek to Oklahoma, the stampede into this rich farmland had begun. Clear springs bubbling out of a holly grove were a prime discovery, quickly drawing a tavern and a few rude log huts. By early 1835, enough newcomers had stopped here to warrant the formation of a town.

New towns don't create themselves; it always takes someone with vision and initiative to see the potential for a community. Whitnel Sephas Randolph was a West Tennessee trader with his eye on the opportunities developing in north Mississippi. He pulled together a consortium with nineteen other men to develop a town site in Marshall County. The legislature had decreed that the county seat must be within five miles of the county's geographic center, and Holly Springs fit that bill perfectly. In the fall of 1835, advertisements were running in newspapers extolling the virtues of the settlement.

Randolph and his cohorts had opened the floodgates. Within months of its formation, Holly Springs had a population of 4,000, making it the third largest city in the state behind Natchez and Columbus. Hugh Craft, an agent for the American Land Company, was sent in to settle claims for the government. He set up shop in a small Greek Revival cottage off the square and worked frantically to keep up with the deluge of land-hungry newcomers.

Many of the early Holly Springs settlers were from old, established families in the Carolinas, Georgia and Virginia. They were accustomed to a high standard of living and expected no less in this new land. A legitimate courthouse, churches and schools were immediate priorities. The Presbyterians pooled their funds to buy a lot south of the square and put up a mud and pole sanctuary. A log courthouse was built in the center of the square, and citizens gathered in April, 1836, to discuss the creation of a college. Holly Springs was not even officially a city yet when $23,000 was pledged to build a two-story brick school. The intriguingly named Consider Parish was hired to bring the Holly Springs Literary Institute to life. This was a school for boys; the girls would soon study at Holly Springs Female Institute, housed in a handsome Greek Revival mansion which could accommodate 160 boarders.

Holly Springs Literary Institute quickly filled with young men and the trustees petitioned the legislature for its designation as a true collegiate-level school. The legislature, eager to encourage civilized pursuits in these far reaches of the state, concurred. They chartered the institution as "The University of Holly Springs," with "the power to confer all the literary, honorary and scientific degrees." Mississippi's first official university was a reality, housed in an unadorned two-room structure on the western edge of Holly Springs. Its sole building predated the University of Mississippi by almost a decade.

The trustees and supporters of the university were aiming high, but their timing was unfortunate. Classes had scarcely begun in 1839 when a severe financial panic hit Mississippi. Foreclosures and bankruptcy notices filled the newspapers and many who had so ardently supported the new college were forced to renege on their pledges. The trustees sold out to the Methodist Conference, which tried valiantly to carry forward the goals of the school. Ambitious plans included a medical school and law school, but by 1843 the entire college had closed.

Begun with such promise just five years earlier, Holly Springs in the early

This deteriorated brick structure housed Mississippi's first chartered public college, the University of Holly Springs. That school failed, but the building would later be home to Chalmers Institute, a prestigious boys' school.

The Stephenson-McAlexander House, a Greek Revival cottage built around 1850 in the community of Mack, five miles north of Holly Springs. A sweeping curve still evident in the highway was designed to miss the garden of Major J. P. M. Stephenson.

1840s didn't seem to have much more of a future than did its university. The economic picture was bleak, cotton prices were low and two of the three local banks had failed. Many townspeople bailed out, heading on to new frontiers in Texas. Those who stayed and rode out the bad times to the end of the decade saw Marshall County once again flourishing. Prosperity in antebellum Mississippi rose and fell with the cotton crop, and by 1850 Marshall was producing more cotton than any other county in the state. A more substantial courthouse had replaced the early log cabin; it was an impressive structure with two floors rising from a foundation of native stone and capped with an octagonal dome over a copper roof. Greek Revival mansions, built with cotton money, lined the streets and dotted the countryside.

Cotton dominated the agricultural fortunes of north Mississippi, but an occasional adventuresome planter branched out a bit. Major J. P. M. Stephenson added a vast fruit orchard on his plantation north of Holly Springs, expanding it to 10,000 trees. His business provided the funds for a gracious Greek Revival home, one-and-a-half stories with a columned portico. A separate kitchen was attached to the house by a rear gallery, and cast-iron oval ventilators were interspersed along the brick foundation. Numerous outbuildings supported the home, the most notable being an office built to match the style of the house, right down to identical ventilators.

Holly Springs was fulfilling its original promise. Cotton prices were high again and the gins ran day and night throughout the fall. Even the old university building had new life; it reopened in 1847 as Chalmers Institute under the leadership of Presbyterian cleric Samuel McKinney. Through a succession of owners, the school expanded to include a military division and the building was enlarged to include more classrooms.

All Holly Springs lacked in 1850 was a reliable means of transport. The nearest navigable river was the Tallahatchie, twenty miles to the south, and Memphis was the closest cotton market. Getting cotton to market was an arduous and dangerous task and traveling for pleasure was all but impossible. Holly Springs needed a railroad. A group including Judge J. W. Clapp and Colonel Harvey Washington Walter trekked to New Orleans to seek support for a line connecting north Mississippi with the Crescent City. Potential investors were impressed with the figures Clapp and Walter brandished, demonstrating the amount of cotton which would leave the Memphis market and put money in New Orleans pockets. With enthusiasm on both ends of the deal, the Mississippi Central Railroad was chartered in 1852. Engineers fanned out to begin surveying the route; ground was broken for the railroad and a Holly Springs depot in October, 1852. Jones and McIlwain Foundry, a local factory best known for its detail work on Holly Springs mansions, was pressed into service to manufacture rails. Other rails were shipped from Europe, transferred to steamboats in New Orleans and sent upriver to Memphis. From there they were carted by wagon down to Holly Springs.

By 1855, the rail lines winding north from Canton were nearing those headed south from Holly Springs. Two locomotives arrived from Massachusetts, enormous coal-powered engines covered with brass and gold leaf and dubbed "H. W. Walter" and "Joseph Collins" in honor of two men instrumental in building the railroad. In May, 1855, the last spike was driven at Winona and "Joseph Collins" fired up its boilers. It steamed south out of

In the late 1800s, this combination train station/hotel was the most popular night spot in north Mississippi, with excursion trains running daily from Memphis. It was converted into a private home in the 1940s.

Over the course of the Civil War, Holly Springs would change hands no less than 62 times, leaving it in shambles.

Holly Springs, and the Mississippi Central Railroad was officially in business. Within two years, two passenger trains were coming from the north and two from the south each day. Travellers streamed in and out of a large depot, which quickly became a popular gathering spot in Holly Springs.

If war had not come to Mississippi, Holly Springs' new prominence on the railroad circuit would have continued to serve it well. But war did come, and when it reached north Mississippi in late 1862, Holly Springs was in the eye of the storm. The same rail lines that brought dozens of visitors into town each day made Holly Springs the ideal spot for a Federal supply depot. When General U. S. Grant first set his sights on capturing Vicksburg, his plan was to march his army across Mississippi and attack it from the east. To support such an effort, he had to have a secure supply base with rail connections. Holly Springs was a sitting duck with its shiny new tracks. Grant swept into town, commandeered the train station and depot, lined Courthouse Square with ammunition and food supplies and politely (or not so politely) moved families out of the mansions so his officers could plan the invasion of Mississippi in comfort. Holly Springs was occupied territory.

There wasn't much the townspeople could do about soldiers in their businesses and homes, but they were truly shocked when Union horses were stabled in the new Presbyterian Church. The fourth building for that congregation had been started one block south of the square in 1858, its elaborate brickwork and pews constructed mainly by the slaves belonging to members of the church. When war halted work on the structure, the basement and exterior walls were complete, but the sanctuary was not yet ready for services. Union soldiers made a token visit to Sunday services and then took over the incomplete building. Horses were led into the basement and munitions were stored in the sanctuary. Lumber intended for pews was instead fashioned into coffins. For a few weeks, as the troops rested before continuing their southward trek, they relieved their boredom by shooting holes in the twenty-inch-thick bricks of the front façade.

In early December, Grant began the march south toward Vicksburg, leaving a skeleton staff in Holly Springs to guard his supplies. Grant had ordered supply trains loaded and stoked on the Mississippi Central tracks, with an engine on each end of the train ready to head north or south as the need warranted. At 3:00 a.m. on the morning of December 20, 1862, startled Holly Springs residents were awakened by the sound of gunfire, explosions and rebel yells as exuberant Confederates caught the Northern sentries sleeping. The trains were blown up in a tremendous shower of sparks and wood, littering the town with uncut U. S. dollars from the paymaster's car. Tons of food and ammunition were set ablaze on the square. The congregation of the Presbyterian Church, knowing that their sanctuary was packed with volatile munitions, prayed that the flames coming off the square wouldn't set the church off, leveling the entire town. Fortunately, the fire never reached the church, and the horses were moved out to more suitable stables when the excitement died down. Van Dorn's raid was successful and the town was back in Confederate hands.

Grant was furious at the loss of his supply line, and his army retaliated by laying waste to north Mississippi. Railroad ties were pulled from the

The original Marshall County Courthouse was accidentally destroyed by Union troops during one of their many occupations of Holly Springs. This 1870 replacement was extensively remodeled in 1929.

ground, heated and then wrapped around trees. The Confederates would not hold Holly Springs for long; over the course of the remaining 2½ years of war, the town would change hands no less than 62 times, leaving it in shambles. By war's end, the courthouse and Holly Springs Female Institute had burned, along with much of the square. The Depot was intact but in bad shape when its telegraph wires relayed an April, 1865, message: "Hell's to pay, Lee's surrendered."

Reconstruction was slow and hard for Holly Springs. The courthouse was rebuilt under a Republican government. The architectural firm of Willis, Sloan and Trigg designed an impressive Italianate brick building with arched windows and heavy brackets underneath the eaves.

Chalmers Institute had struggled through the war by cutting back on its staff and enrollment. Several of its students, alumni and at least one faculty member were killed in the conflict. In 1869, it entered one of its most successful decades under the leadership of Professor William Anderson. A spirited competition developed with neighboring St. Thomas Hall, an Episcopal military academy, for the brightest students.

General Absalom Madden West had taken control over what was left of the Mississippi Central Railroad in 1864. His task was monumental; all but a few miles of railbed was ruined. Mules were pulling railroad cars from Oxford. It would take years of backbreaking labor and thousands of dollars to rebuild the line and replace hundreds of cars which had been destroyed during the war.

The Presbyterian congregation may have understandably felt that only divine intervention had brought their incomplete church through the war years. The question now was how to complete the building; many fortunes had been lost during the war and most folks had their hands full just putting food on their tables. Reverend H. H. Paine embarked on a cross-country trek through the North and Midwest, appealing to the sympathy (or guilt) of fellow Presbyterians nationwide. He raised enough money to return home and oversee the finishing touches. By 1869, the long-awaited Bohemian stained-glass windows were in place and the sanctuary completed. A cast-iron crested ogee arch was placed over the bullet-riddled front doors.

Slowly, Holly Springs recovered from the turmoil of war and Reconstruction. The local government was back in Democratic hands by 1875, and the fire-damaged sides of the square were reconstructed. Chalmers Institute and St. Thomas Hall were waging a lively battle for the young men of the community. Several schools opened for the education of freed slaves, including Shaw University (which would become Rust College), Baptist Negro College and the State Normal School for Negroes. The Depot had been rebuilt and once again a few trains were running on the relaid tracks. But just as people were beginning to feel that better days had returned for good, Holly Springs would once again have to deal with a disaster.

Yellow fever epidemics were a yearly occurrence in Mississippi. They were much more common in low-lying, swampy areas where the mosquito vector thrived, and Holly Springs had been spared serious outbreaks in its fifty-year history. In 1878, a particularly bad epidemic ravaged many towns in Mississippi, including Grenada. Tragically assuming that their "healthful air" insulated them from infection, Holly Springs' concerned citizens opened their doors to Grenada refugees. Within days, the first local victim succumbed in the little house where Hugh Craft had once managed land deeds. The infection spread like wildfire through town, and streets leading to the Depot were clogged with horses and wagons, their occupants desperate to find a place on the last trains to leave before Holly Springs was quarantined. Before the fall's first frost brought an end to the suffering, 1,400 Holly Springs residents had fallen ill and more than 300 were dead. The epidemic was no respecter of

Cathrine Hall was the first of several elegant Jacobean Revival structures to be built on the campus of Mississippi Industrial College, Bishop Elias Cockrell's school for black youths. The dormitory incorporated an antebellum planter's mansion.

wealth or power. Colonel Harvey Walter and several of his family members died in their castle-like mansion, Walter Place. Twelve Catholic nuns stayed behind to care for the sick after evacuating their Bethlehem Academy students; six would die of yellow fever. Chalmers Institute was hard-hit, and the school closed for good not long after the epidemic.

Despite the setback of epidemic, the final twenty years of the nineteenth century were good ones for Holly Springs. The rebuilt Mississippi Central Railroad was absorbed by the Illinois Central system, and in 1886 the great Victorian Depot was built around the remains of two earlier depots. Dominating the east end of Holly Springs with its steep roof and triple towers, the combination train station and hotel was the hot spot of Holly Springs' social scene for many years. Excursion trains brought carloads of revelers from Memphis, who would book accommodations in one of the hotel's twenty bedrooms and dance the night away in the grand ballroom. A French chef from New Orleans was imported to run the kitchen, and huge vats behind the building turned out carbide gas to keep the lights running through the night. A six-mule trolley pulled a fifty-passenger bus from the square to the depot and back several times a day.

As the century ended, Holly Springs found itself facing one more hurdle, one which would be more long-lasting and insurmountable than war or political turmoil or disease. The local farmland, thinned by sixty years of demanding cotton production, was washing away like sand. Levees and drained swamps had made the Delta into the state's new cotton kingdom, and the boll weevil's arrival in 1906 all but wiped out the remaining agricultural economy in Marshall County. Holly Springs' growth years were over.

In an ironic juxtaposition of the old and the new, Mississippi Industrial

Chancellor F.A.P. Barnard may have designed the observatory for the fledgling University of Mississippi himself. The world's largest astronomical lens was being ground for the observatory but was never delivered to Oxford.

thrown together on the square. The financial panic of 1837 marked the end of many neighboring towns as their founders headed for new lands in Texas; Oxford was protected from extinction by its status as county seat. When the economy recovered, businesses located on the square and a new, more permanent courthouse was planned. Soon after the courthouse's completion, Oxford landed another prize. Seven towns around Mississippi had waged a fierce competition in the chambers of Jackson's new Capitol for the proposed University of Mississippi. Kosciusko, Louisville, Mississippi City, Middleton, Brandon and Monroe Missionary Station were hardly more than crossroads, much like Oxford, but all were willing to commit property and financial backing to secure a college. Oxford edged out Mississippi City by one vote and began planning for an institution to rival its English namesake.

The usual legislative wrangling over funding would delay the opening of the university until 1848, but Oxford's future was secure. When the U. S. government designated it as the site of a federal court, lawyers and legal workers poured into town. Cotton was fueling the agricultural economy, and in 1850 Lafayette County boasted more than a thousand farms and plantations.

By 1848, state architect William Nichols had completed the Greek Revival Lyceum building in the center of the university's site. Two dorms, a steward's hall and several professors' cottages completed the campus. Classes began in November of that year, with eighty freshmen and sophomores enrolling. Forty-seven would complete the year, and the following session saw their numbers rise to 232.

Five years later, Frederick A. P. Barnard, a renowned University of Alabama astronomy professor, was lured to Oxford as president of the state's rapidly growing flagship institution. Barnard was a man of enthusiastic visions, and he fully intended to transform this fledgling college into a world-class mecca for scientific experimentation and study. He badgered the legis-

The financial panic of 1837 marked the end of many neighboring towns, but Oxford was protected from extinction by its status as county seat.

lature endlessly, extracting funds to build his dreams into reality. The cornerstone of his plan was an "Astronomical Observatory," patterned after the pacesetting structures at Harvard and in Poulkova, Russia. The farmers and backwoods lawyers of the legislature were overwhelmed by this Yale graduate and his persistent ideas, and they allocated the phenomenal sum of $20,000 to fund the project.

Barnard designed and oversaw the 1857-1859 construction of a huge, three-sectioned observatory and classroom building. When completed, lecture halls, labs and spacious living quarters for Barnard were included. Rising above the structure were three huge turrets, the center one intended to hold what would be the world's largest astronomical lens. A nineteen-inch lens was ordered from the Cambridge, Massachusetts firm of Alvan Clark and Sons, and Barnard eagerly waited for the grinding process to be completed.

Astronomy wasn't Chancellor Barnard's only heavenly interest. He was also an ordained Episcopal priest and in 1856 he was chosen as the first full-time rector of tiny St. Peter's parish. The church was growing along with Oxford, and it was seen by the bishop as being particularly essential in a town

The new Lafayette County courthouse was designed by Holly Springs architect Spires Boling in 1870. Plans to tear it down in the 1940s inspired a furious "letter-to-the-editor" from William Faulkner.

with so many impressionable students. By the late 1850s, the parishioners were ready to build a permanent church; they chose a design by famed ecclesiastical architect Richard Upjohn. A brick chapel was completed in 1860, and Barnard preached the first sermon in the new sanctuary in April of that year.

As Oxford developed into a prosperous town, its architecture reflected the wealth and success of its merchants, lawyers and planters. Two remarkable homes would anchor opposite ends of town. Jacob Thompson was an early arrival in the Chickasaw cession, serving as its congressman from 1839 until 1851. When he lost his seat in the 1851 elections, he moved his considerable wealth to Oxford and built a twenty-room Greek Revival mansion on the southern edge of town. Still active in national politics, Thompson was persuaded by President James Buchanan to serve as his Secretary of the Interior in 1856.

On the opposite side of Oxford, planter Thomas Pegues was building an Italianate masterpiece to rival the Thompson mansion. Pegues had come to Oxford from South Carolina and amassed a fortune, including 4,000 acres of farmland and over 150 slaves. When he was ready to build a house on his Oxford land, he travelled to New York to discuss designs with Calvert Vaux, an English architect who collaborated with Frederick Law Olmstead to create New York City's Central Park. Vaux drew up a complete set of elevations for the Pegues House, and work began in 1859. Pegues had seen to it that the road from the courthouse square to his house would be pleasant, planting oaks along both sides of the thoroughfare.

1861 found workers busy on the Pegues House and Chancellor Barnard anxiously awaiting the arrival of his cherished lens from Massachusetts.

The Thomas Pegues house, Ammadelle, was designed by Calvert Vaux, one of the architects of New York's Central Park. Charred floorboards are still visible in an upstairs bedroom, reminders of the Union rampage through Oxford in 1864.

Nationally, tension was rising; South Carolina had seceded from the Union and Mississippi followed her lead in January. Barnard saw certain disaster for Mississippi and the university if war came. The campus was overrun with hot-headed young men, their minds preoccupied with getting into battle as soon as possible. Barnard's desperate pleas for reason were drowned out in the tumult.

U. S. President James Buchanan complicated matters by sending a supply ship, the *Star of the West,* to reinforce Fort Sumter. Interior Secretary Jacob Thompson fired off a telegram to South Carolina's governor, advising him to "blow the *Star of the West* out of the water" and then resigned his cabinet post and hurried south to Oxford. Heading the other way was Barnard, scheduled to lecture at the Smithsonian Institute. In his absence, his students formed the University Greys and marched off to oblivion. Mississippi was gearing for war, not stargazing, and Barnard's long-awaited lens was diverted to Northwestern University. He knew his days in the observatory were numbered; even his parishioners at St. Peter's were whispering about his suspect loyalties. Jacob Thompson defended his pastor vociferously, but to no avail. Barnard resigned from the university and St. Peter's and sadly headed north, his dream of a great university dashed by forces beyond his control. In 1864, he would take over the presidency of King's College, New York, and build it into Columbia University.

Only four students showed up at the university for classes in the fall of 1861. The school closed, and Barnard Observatory and the Lyceum were converted into hospitals for hundreds of dying soldiers from numerous battles across Mississippi. War reached Oxford in late 1862, as General Grant marched south from Holly Springs toward Vicksburg. Union tents were pitched on the courthouse lawn; they were hastily taken down when word came of Confederate General Earl Van Dorn's predawn raid on Holly Springs. All was relatively quiet in Oxford until 1864, when the conflict

Chancellor Barnard served as the first priest of St. Peter's Episcopal Church in 1860. His northern sentiments were viewed with suspicion by many parishioners, and he resigned from the church and the university the following year.

In 1887, the crowning touch to the rebuilt Oxford square was added in the form of the Richardsonian Romanesque Federal Building and Post Office.

returned in its later, more vindictive phase.

In 1864, Mississippi was essentially a conquered state, and Union occupation was the rule for most towns. General A. J. "Whiskey" Smith's troops patrolled Lafayette County, and some unknown insult set them off on a terrifying rampage. Jacob Thompson's house was a logical target. Thompson was in Canada on a secret mission for Jefferson Davis; General Smith drove the family from the house and torched it. He did nothing to stop his men from storming into downtown Oxford, setting the courthouse and the surrounding businesses on fire; even the Presbyterian church was engulfed. They swarmed up the roads north of the square, reaching the incomplete shell of the Pegues House. Soldiers were putting their torches to a second-floor bedroom when Confederate guns were heard in the distance. The troops fled, leaving charred and blackened planks on the floor. One observer, standing in the ruins of Oxford, described it as "the most completely demolished town [I] have seen anywhere."

The university buildings and St. Peter's were spared, perhaps because of Chancellor Barnard's northern connections. But the heart of Oxford was gone; only one warehouse on the square survived the blaze. As the war ended, Oxonians faced another ten years of military occupation, and they slowly rebuilt through Reconstruction and the years that followed. Jacob Thompson fled to Europe, waiting for a more forgiving political climate to prevail. When he did return to Oxford, he built a more modest home for his son on the site of his lost mansion and then moved to Memphis.

Even in its devastated state, Oxford was still the county seat and a new courthouse was going to be necessary. Spires Boling of Holly Springs was hired as the architect, and the new building rose on the ashes of the old one.

Its three stories of stuccoed brick and four-faced clock tower would come to symbolize Oxford. The north and south façades were complemented with pedimented porticoes and Corinthian columns rising from masonry arches.

St. Peter's survived the war with minimal damage and was finally consecrated in 1871. A towering spire was added in 1893, and it achieved the appearance it would carry through the next century.

The Pegues House was completed during Reconstruction, with only minor adjustments to Vaux's detailed plans. The charred floorboards upstairs were left as a reminder of the house's darkest day. When it came into the possession of Ben Price, he named the home "Ammadelle" in honor of his wife and sister.

The University of Mississippi reopened and slowly rebuilt its student population. The slim funds meted out by the legislature were not intended for such frivolous items as telescope lenses, and the turret machinery in Barnard Observatory rusted from disuse. The building was divided into two sections, the east half serving as the Chancellor's residence and the west half as classrooms for physics and astronomy.

A recent addition to the old Federal Building is a statue of William Faulkner, posed on one of his favorite benches.

Twenty years passed before businesses on the square filled in the gaps left from the devastating fire of 1864. Most were built of brick with shed roofs and porches supported by cast iron columns. The crowning touch to the square came from the same Federal government whose armies had laid waste to Oxford's downtown. In 1887, a massive red brick Federal Building and Post Office, designed in the popular Richardsonian Romanesque style, was completed northeast of the courthouse.

Twentieth-century Oxford could have been any of a hundred small county seats throughout the South. Its courthouse dominated downtown, surrounded by small businesses and a lawn full of farmers and old men on any given Saturday. Radiating away from the square, the streets were lined by Thomas Pegues' oaks and graced with a pleasing assortment of antebellum mansions and Victorian cottages. This was a typical Southern town, but it was destined for worldwide renown as William Faulkner's fictional "Jefferson." Each year, scholars and avid readers would walk the streets of Oxford looking for the inspiration in Faulkner's Yoknapatawpha County. They would visit St. Peter's, where Faulkner took an occasional Sunday morning seat, and study the faces on the courthouse lawn for signs of a Snopes or a Sartoris. Some would be versed enough in the legends of Oxford to know that a furious " letter-to-the-editor" from Faulkner in 1947 helped prevent demolition of the courthouse. His home, Rowan Oak, was just across the road from the site of Jacob Thompson's long-vanished home.

Faulkner immortalized Oxford in fiction, but even his inventive mind could not conceive a story sadder than Frederick Barnard's ill-fated sojourn in Mississippi. By 1990, the observatory was crumbling, having been used in turn as a sorority house, a Navy ROTC center and finally left to the elements as a worn-out anachronism. There seemed little use for a 130-year-old monument to unfulfilled dreams. But in an ending worthy of a Nobel novelist, the observatory was rescued at the last minute to become the Center for the Study of Southern Culture. Its rickety turrets were stabilized, the interior was restored to full glory, and the halls again echoed with students and professors.

Frederick Barnard and William Faulkner would no doubt have much to say about southern culture as an academic discipline. Barnard saw a stubborn devotion to tradition destroy the potential of an entire generation, and Faulkner wove that same sense of place and family throughout his thought-provoking novels. Oxford reflects those conflicts in its history, its architecture and its status as an academic and literary mecca.

Yazoo City

Ricks Memorial
Library

Hanan's Bluff was the only place in the entire Mississippi Delta river system where the Yazoo curved east and touched the Loess Bluffs. It was here that speculators plotted a town on land purchased from Choctaw chief Greenwood Leflore.

*Y*azoo City exists in two distinct worlds. Half occupies the tip of the Delta, with perfectly flat streets lacking even a hillock from one block to the next. The other half seems to rise straight up out of that Delta, twisting and curving along the bluffs that abruptly signal an end to the flatlands. In their heavily wooded old neighborhoods, the two worlds can jut right up against each other from one yard to the next.

There are high points in and around Yazoo City where the juxtaposition of Delta and Hills is dramatic and memorable. One is Bell Road, an ancient trail carved out of the soft loess bluffs and trod down until its roadbed lies twenty feet beneath the surrounding surface. Bells were hung around the necks of oxen following its sharp twists and turns, warning fellow travellers of traffic coming the other direction and giving it its name. Walking down Bell Road today is almost an eerie experience. Cars are few, and the silence is heightened by the shade of trees fallen from one edge of the bluff to the other, their exposed roots desperately hanging on to the shifting dirt. Occasionally, the bluffs recede, leaving a view over the Delta that stretches forever. A similar view is found at the very top of Glenwood Cemetery, resting place of many of the memorable characters who built Yazoo City. From this vantage point, the bayou snaking its way down Canal Street and the redoubts where Civil War battles were fought are clearly evident. Just as on Bell Road, the view to the west is nothing but Delta all the way to the horizon.

Yazoo City exists because of Hanan's Bluff. That ferry crossing was the only place where the twisting waters of the Tallahatchie-Yazoo River system

Bell Road, an ancient road from Yazoo City to Vicksburg, was worn down through the soft loess soil by thousands of horses and oxcarts. With its narrow, blind curves being so treacherous, bells were hung around the animals' necks to warn other travellers of oncoming traffic.

crept back to touch the line of hills running from Memphis to Vicksburg. When Choctaw Chief Greenwood Leflore signed the Treaty of Doak's Stand in 1820, the grateful U. S. government gave him his choice of land as a reward. One section which he eagerly snatched up was the square mile encompassing Hanan's Bluff. Perhaps it had some symbolic meaning for the Choctaw nation; more likely, the ever-enterprising Leflore saw it as a means of making a quick dollar. It was formally granted to him in February, 1826; by April of that year, he had sold it for ten dollars an acre to three speculators. Land changed hands quickly in those days, often unseen by its temporary owners, and this choice spot soon found its way to a group of five men, calling themselves the "Proprietors of Clinton." Among them were Hiram Runnels, a future governor of Mississippi, and Isaac Caldwell, a state legislator whose propensity for settling disputes on the dueling field would cost him his life.

The "Proprietors" were nothing if not good real estate salesmen; they platted out a town to be called "Manchester" and advertised the sale of lots far and wide: "Manchester is situated on a high and beautiful bluff . . . affords a suitable and safe landing for steam boats at all stages of the water . . . this is the only suitable point known in a high stage of the water for one hundred and fifty miles above Manchester or about thirty miles below." The steamboat *Octavia* was chartered to ferry potential buyers up from cash-rich Natchez. On February 22, 1830, the landing at Manchester was crowded with eager settlers and speculators with ready checkbooks. Before the day was out, one hundred and twelve lots had been sold. Manchester was a reality.

By 1834, every lot in Manchester was claimed. Stores sprang up quickly along Main Street, which curved from the base of the hills to the river. They supplied goods for the influx of townspeople and the plantation owners on the edge of the Delta. Grey and Henry Vick, heirs of Vicksburg's founder, bought up several hundred acres of land just north of Manchester for Lintonia Plantation. By 1839, the little town on the hills had grown to over a thousand people, and the name was changed to Yazoo City in recognition of the river which gave it birth. One of the first to make his fortune there was Samuel Wilson, a jeweler who somehow made his way south from Susquehanna, Pennsylvania in 1841. Planters and steamboat owners must have kept his business humming; by 1846, he was building an enormous white mansion on Madison Street for his wife. Yazoo County had no natural source of stone and its porous clay soil was less than optimal for bricks, so most of its fine antebellum houses, like the Wilson House, were frame. The elements of the house were pre-cut in Cincinnati, loaded on a barge and shipped downriver to Vicksburg, then upriver to Yazoo City. The boards were pegged together without nails.

The 1850s saw a steady stream of riverboat traffic docking at the end of Main Street, unloading passengers and picking up the cotton which poured in from all over north and central Mississippi. Yazoo City was one of the South's most prosperous inland ports, and its superior location made it a natural site for one of the Confederacy's three naval yards when war came. It was never much of an operation, just a few machine shops and blacksmith sheds, but one of the Civil War's most memorable naval battles would be fought with a ship built here.

In the summer of 1862, Admiral David Farragut's fleet was sitting in the Mississippi River, pestering the fortifications on the bluffs at Vicksburg. The only hope of the outnumbered and outclassed Confederate Navy seemed to rest in the development of ironclads, clunky gunboats outfitted with metal

Jeweler Samuel Wilson emigrated to Mississippi from Pennsylvania and accumulated enough wealth to build one of Yazoo City's grandest mansions, the Wilson-Gilruth House. A Confederate drummer boy, brazenly waving his grey cap from the balcony at Union soldiers marching by, was shot and nearly killed for his efforts.

Yazoo City was one of the South's most prosperous inland ports, and its superior location made it a natural site for one of the Confederacy's three naval yards when war came.

cladding above the water line. The *Arkansas* was a thrown-together wreck of a ship which had been sitting idle in the Yazoo River above Greenwood. Yazoo Naval Yard Commander Isaac Brown knew it had no engines or plating; nevertheless, given a mandate to "finish and quip (sic) that vessel without regard to expenditure of men or money," Brown towed it to Yazoo City and set his crews to work. Two hundred men labored around the clock to bolt on armor-plating, using anything remotely resembling metal. Railroad ties and boiler plate were cobbled together with rivets, and two badly unbalanced engines were installed beneath the decks. Guns were mounted, and in July, the strangest ship to ever steam past Yazoo City left the Naval Yard. Her inexperienced sailors had to contend with engines so mismatched that the ship had a tendency to spin in circles. The Union fleet was only fifty miles away, leaving precious little time to practice steering the ramshackle warboat. Once it rounded a bend near the mouth of the Yazoo, it was do or die. A Union officer described the bizarre sight sailing into his path: ". . . the monster shoved around the point, and a moment later, her huge form lay clearly exposed as all alone she headed boldly towards the whole fleet . . . and it was evident there was mischief in her . . . She seemed more impregnable than the *Merrimac,* the terror whose name still filled the land."

The *Arkansas* would wreak havoc for several days in the Mississippi River, damaging or sinking a number of Union gunboats. She blew up en route to

out as Fifteenth Street. In 1921, the tracks were covered over and the cars sold to the city of Helena, Arkansas.

Streetcars weren't the only form of transportation which twentieth-century progress would render useless. Railroads and highways had replaced the need for waterways, and the Yazoo River saw less and less traffic. Floods were a predictable spring occurrence in downtown Yazoo, and the 1927 Great Mississippi River Flood left Main Street inundated. It was time to reroute the stream which had once been the reason for Yazoo City's very existence. The U. S. Army Corps of Engineers dammed and dynamited and turned the channel into a new bed, far from town, leaving only an oxbow lake at the foot of Main Street.

Changes were coming all over town. On Madison Street, the Wilson-Gilruth House went through a period as a medical clinic and hospital before being converted back into a private residence. The Oakes House gradually declined and decayed, nearly crumbling before the Yazoo County Fair and Civic League undertook its restoration as an African-American Cultural Center. Main Street School served Yazoo's students for seventy-two years before obsolescence caught up with it in 1976. With a thousand memories echoing in its hallways, it was too valuable to abandon altogether. The Triangle Cultural Center was formed to establish a local museum and archives, and the top floor now holds the history of Yazoo County. Next door, the Ricks Memorial Library has outlasted all of its contemporaries, achieving the honor of being the oldest active library in Mississippi. Its circular main room still glows with "an abundance of light" pouring through plate glass windows, and the multicolored skylight over the circulation desk shines like new. The portrait of Mrs. Ricks (complete with borrowed hair style) hangs prominently by the front door.

Along Grand Avenue lies Circle Park, donated to the city by Fanny Ricks.

Walking to the crest of Glenwood Cemetery, you pass General and Mrs. Ricks' graves, not far from that of Colonel Gilruth. Back in the Jewish section is a marker honoring Willie Wise, possibly the very one who started the Great Fire of 1904. From the crest of the graveyard, the view of the Delta is uninterrupted, stretching away to the horizon. Cutting across it like a dark ribbon is the Yazoo River, whose turn toward the hills gave rise to the town which would carry its name across the years.

Carrollton

Carrollton Methodist Church

*I*n 1968, Hollywood came looking for Mississippi. Jefferson, Mississippi, circa 1904, to be exact. William Faulkner's last novel, the light-hearted *Reivers,* was headed for the big screen, and the producers figured it would be much easier to use an existing town rather than build one from scratch in California. Jefferson's alter-ego, Oxford, had become too modernized to serve their purposes. A small Mississippi town with a courthouse square, unchanged over the course of a century, was what they needed.

What they found was Carrollton. A few truckloads of dirt were spread on the streets, a plywood front transformed the town's only gas station into a livery stable, and Jefferson, Mississippi was reborn. Carrollton, long past its days as a bustling market town, had been rediscovered.

Carroll County was one of the areas carved out of the 1830's Treaty of Dancing Rabbit Creek. It was a huge county, stretching from deep in the Delta up into the loess bluff hills. No one in their rational mind risked the malarial air and humid summers of the Delta, so naturally the county seat would be up in the hills. Forty acres along the south side of Big Sand Creek was designated as "Carrollton" and the town was under way. Lots were sold in the summer of 1835 and a small courthouse built on the square.

Carrollton rapidly developed into a legitimate town. The Delta was producing its early bumper crops of cotton, but very few planters wanted to live there. They took their cotton money up Valley Hill to Carrollton, filling the lots with columned mansions and townhouses. Businesses opened on the square to meet their needs. On the south side of the square, a row of brick

This 1880s structure, the old jail, is an exuberant example of a community necessity.

J. Z. George had this six-sided library constructed on the front lawn of his 1830s mansion, Cotesworth. He relied extensively on its law books as he labored to write the Mississippi Constitution of 1890, still in use today.

Merrill's Store is the only remaining building from a block of mercantile establishments which once stood south of the courthouse. It has served as a general store, the county courtroom and a coffin factory.

storefronts known as Tobin Row included Merrill's Store, a millinery and a bakery.

When the Indian treaties were signed, the Choctaws were each given the option of staying and claiming 640 acres of land. Very few did. They left behind their last chief, Greenwood Leflore, a crafty negotiator who came away from Dancing Rabbit Creek owning thousands of acres stretching from Carroll County to Yazoo City. Leflore was only one-quarter Choctaw, born in 1800 to Frenchman Louis LeFleur and Rebecca Cravat, the niece of Chief Pushmataha. He had grown up at LeFleur's Bluff (which would become Jackson) and French Camp. As a teenager, he was taken to Nashville for a formal education by Major Donley, a family friend who owned the Natchez Trace mail concession.

Leflore returned to Mississippi as a young man with Donley's daughter as his bride, a well-rounded education and a flair for leadership which would elevate him to to the top of the Choctaw nation in the 1820s. He realized early on that the few white settlers in north Mississippi would soon become hundreds. At Dancing Rabbit Creek, he signed the papers which began his people's long trek to Oklahoma and personally came away with the nucleus of one of Mississippi's antebellum empires. Leflore was a major figure in Carroll County politics for years, winning election to the state legislature soon after the county was formed. In Jackson, he gained notoriety for his impatience with the pompous legislators who gave long, boring Latin orations on the Capitol floor. Rising to speak on some obscure topic, Leflore held forth for an hour in fluent Choctaw. The Latin speeches stopped.

By the mid-1850s, Greenwood Leflore had built an empire on his Teoc Plantation. Four hundred slaves worked his cotton fields and he had personally financed the construction of a road across the Delta to Point Leflore. He was ready to replace his log house with "Malmaison," a fifteen-room mansion

At Dancing Rabbit Creek, Choctaw chief Greenwood Leflore signed the papers which began his people's long trek to Oklahoma and came away with the nucleus of one of Mississippi's antebellum empires.

designed by Georgia architect James Clark Harris. Malmaison would be built of cypress wood cut and seasoned for a year on Teoc's grounds. Combining the Greek Revival and Italianate styles which dominated Mississippi's late antebellum architecture, Malmaison was as visually stunning as any of the famous houses of Natchez or Columbus. The interior featured two long hallways intersecting in a Maltese cross and ten-foot-tall doorways. The rooms were furnished with mahogany furniture, Aubusson carpets and hand-painted draperies, all imported from France. An entire wing was devoted to a 60-foot-long dining room; its eighteen-foot-long table held a French china service for 100 and 12 dozen place settings of silver.

Leflore's days at Malmaison were short-lived. The Civil War brought the cotton kingdom to an end, and Leflore's outspoken Unionist sentiments didn't sit well with his Carroll County neighbors. Having no railroad, waterways or factories to be fought over, Carrollton missed the war completely. Friction still ran high in the county. Leflore flew the Union flag from the high cupola of Malmasion throughout the war, and more than once his servants had to extinguish fires set at Malmaison by his angry neighbors. He would die just after the war ended, buried in the U. S. flag in Malmaison's cemetery.

Carrollton's distance from the war led to a faster economic and social recovery than in other parts of Mississippi. The 1870s did bring a reduction in the size of the county, as Leflore, Montgomery and Grenada counties were

All that remains of Malmaison are scattered mounds of bricks and a few stone steps. A short walk north of the house site is the family cemetery where the Choctaw chief and many of his children are buried.

As the Delta built up and cotton again brought wealth into the area, Carrollton served as an important commercial and government center.

James Clark Harris designed this 1878 replacement for the first Carroll County Courthouse, which had been torched by an angry voter. The total cost of the new building was $9,000.

carved out in 1871. Greenwood Leflore was gone, but Carrollton didn't lack for political influence. James Z. George, a lawyer who had immigrated from Georgia in 1836 and gained admittance to Mississippi's bar at the age of 20, was a rising star in Reconstruction Mississippi. In 1847, George had purchased a two-story stagecoach inn on the Grenada Road, naming it "Cotesworth" and rebuilding it into a grand Greek Revival mansion, suitable for his wife and nine children.

George participated in Mississippi's Secession Convention and then went off to war. When he returned, his legal and political skills would serve Mississippi throughout the turbulent late-nineteenth century. In 1875, the state was on the brink of internal war as Democrats wrested control of state offices from the long-dominant Republicans and carpetbaggers. Riots broke out in several cities and Governor Adelbert Ames was threatening to call out the militia, a move which would have surely led to statewide anarchy. George took the lead in convincing Ames to accept the inevitability of Democratic dominance. Ames tendered his resignation and quickly left the state. Order was restored. George went on to serve briefly as Chief Justice of the Mississippi Supreme Court before being elected to the U. S. Senate in 1881.

George's adopted hometown was finding its greatest period of prosperity in the last twenty-five years of the nineteenth century. As the Delta built up and cotton again brought wealth into the area, Carrollton served as an important commercial and governmental center. James Clark Harris had married Greenwood Leflore's daughter and remained in Carroll County after Leflore's death. He would leave a lasting architectural legacy in the area. In 1874, Colonel J. J. Helm hired him to remodel his antebellum Greek Revival house into something larger and more modern. Harris reworked the entrance from the west side to the north, adding a wide porch with elaborate sawn millwork. Numerous outbuildings were designed in fanciful forms, including a smokehouse with a Victorian finial, servants' houses and even a triple-seater privy.

Helm House was originally a much smaller structure which faced west. James Clark Harris, the architect who built Malmaison for Greenwood Leflore, reconstructed it as a Victorian home facing north with numerous fanciful outbuildings.

Another of Harris's projects was the Carroll County Courthouse. Felix Doss had burned down the old one in a fit of anger over election results, and the supervisors contracted with Harris to design a new one. It was finished in 1878, at a cost of $9,000. Its stark simplicity is offset with a typical Harris-designed cupola and pilasters which are vaguely reminiscent of Malmaison. While under construction, Merrill's Store served as the courtroom. On streets leading away from either side of the courthouse square, the Methodist Church and the two-story stuccoed jail also show details suggestive of Harris' work.

In 1880, Carrollton began an unprecedented stretch of direct influence in the U. S. Senate. J. Z. George was serving as Chief Justice of Mississippi's Supreme Court when the legislature chose him to fill one of the state's Senate

Intact outbuildings from the nineteenth century are rare, and Helm House has a remarkable collection in excellent condition. Included are a pigeoneirre and a three-seat outhouse.

seats. He would spend the remaining sixteen years of his life commuting between Carrollton, Washington and Jackson. As his law library and personal papers multiplied, he had plans drawn up for a free-standing library to be built on the front lawn of Cotesworth. The building may or may not have been designed by James Clark Harris; if so, it is an achievement to rank with Malmaison in genius if not in scope. A six-sided roof with a hexagonal glazed cupola tops the six-sided frame building. On the west façade, an entrance porch is framed with pieced millwork and an arched screen set on coupled columns. Inside, six tall bookshelves radiate inward from the walls to the center of the room. Windows set between the bookshelves direct light onto the radiating pattern of the pine floorboards. Directly opposite the doorway, a wooden mantelpiece is painted to resemble marble. George's "Congressional Records" and extensive law library fill the shelves. He relied extensively on those books as he labored to write the Mississippi Constitution of 1890, still in use today.

As Carrollton grew, its small church congregations reached the point where they were ready to build true sanctuaries. Grace Episcopal Church had been organized by Bishop William Mercer Green in 1850, but its members had always met in private homes or shared space with the Presbyterian Church. Its first full-time pastor left for war in 1861, and the church was badly disorganized until the 1880s. In June, 1881, the congregation was reorganized by Reverend W. P. Browne and a building campaign was spearheaded by Sarah Dabney Eggleston and the ladies of the church. They raised $3000 in pledges and contracted with an anonymous architect to build one of Mississippi's most charming small churches. Grace Episcopal is an outstanding example of Gothic Stick style, its gabled roof covered with tin fishscale shingles and crowned on the corner with an open bell tower.

By century's end, Carrollton's population was reaching its all-time popu-

Greenwood has a soul. It's two hundred and ninety feet of steel and rusty machinery, perched atop massive concrete piers. The Keesler Bridge has spanned the always-muddy Yazoo River for three-quarters of a century, linking the historic old streets of downtown with the shady enclaves of North Greenwood. In 1925, boats and barges still plied the waters of the Yazoo, bound for Vicksburg and New Orleans. And when their whistles blew, the bridge had to move. But Keesler was no run-of-the-mill, hinge-in-the-center drawbridge. This span was unique: it turned. All those tons of concrete, steel and superstructure made a sweeping ninety-degree arc into the middle of the Yazoo channel until the ship passed. Then, with a shudder and the grinding of enormous gears, it would slowly shift back into line with Grand Boulevard and Fulton Street. No wonder that offices emptied and windows were thrown open to watch the show whenever a boat approached.

The Keesler Bridge crosses the Yazoo on the site of an earlier, less exciting drawbridge, which had in turn replaced Howell's Ferry in the 1890s. The Yazoo was the Choctaw's "River of Death," where they held their tribal court and carried out ritual executions on the slight rise where Greenwood would be founded. When they reluctantly headed west in 1832, their land was put up for grabs at the going rate of $1.25 an acre. Fifteen thousand of those acres had been claimed by the Choctaw chief, Greenwood Leflore, who negotiated the Treaty of Dancing Rabbit Creek with the U. S. government. Much of his land was considered unusable, deep in the swamps of the Delta with its bears and alligators and snakes. A few speculators and intrepid settlers bought land along the Yazoo, but it did not attract the immediate attention which spawned overnight towns like Holly Springs and Oxford.

Sixteen counties were formed from the Choctaw land; Carroll County was a huge block stretching from the Delta up into the loess bluffs to the east. The legislature designated the little community of Carrollton, safely tucked in the hills, as the county seat. In November, 1834, land grant #6872 of Carroll County was sold to John Williams, encompassing 162 acres along the south bank of the Yazoo River. Williams was undaunted by the hazards along Pelucia Bayou, a small feeder stream which emptied into the Yazoo along an elevated ridge. He saw this as an ideal site for a store, possibly a town, and definitely a shipping point for cotton. He set up shop, selling whiskey and flour, and waited for neighbors to join him. Few did.

One of the Choctaws who remained in Carroll County was Coleman Cole, owner of a large tract of land on both banks of the Yazoo near Williams' property. He sold his holdings to Titus Howard and Samuel B. Marsh, who were a bit more aggressive than Williams in laying out a town. In 1837, they divided their land on the south side of the river into eighty lots and marketed them as "Williams Landing." Within four years, three stores and a tavern faced the river. Carroll County planters found this to be a convenient place to ship their cotton, and Howard and Marsh were working to overcome the reputation of the Delta as an unpleasant, unhealthy place to live. The tiny hamlet of Marion, a few miles downstream, was their only competition, at least until John Williams made a major mistake. He controlled the warehouses where cotton was stored on the river, and he managed to anger one very rich Indian chief.

Greenwood Leflore was among the wealthiest men in Mississippi, owner of 400 slaves. His plantation produced vast quantities of cotton and it was

While hill towns were forming lyceum societies and organizing colleges, Greenwoodians were just intent on surviving day to day without drowning or being eaten by wild beasts.

hauled by wagon to Williams Landing for shipment downriver. History does not record the precise cause of his disagreement with John Williams, but local legend holds that Williams let a large quantity of Leflore's cotton sit in the rain until it was ruined. Whatever the cause, Leflore declared that he would just build his own town; unfortunately for the struggling little town of Williams Landing, he had the resources to do just that. He chose a wooded spit of land where the Yalobusha River flows into the Tallahatchie and both rivers lose their identity in the Yazoo. Leflore immodestly dubbed the site "Point Leflore" and built a sawmill, a brickyard, a hotel and several houses and stores. He poured $75,000 and countless hours of slave labor into the construction of a corduroy road across the muddy Delta and up Valley Hill to his plantation at Teoc.

Temporarily, Leflore was triumphant. Many of the hundred or so flatboats which might dock on a given day at Williams Landing were now venturing a few miles upriver to Point Leflore. But Nature would be the final arbiter of civic supremacy. The Williams Landing site was on a small bluff, providing some measure of protection from the floods which were as predictable as sunrise in the pre-levee Delta. Point Leflore may have had the advantage of three rivers at its doorstep, but when those rivers rose, the folly of Greenwood Leflore's dream was evident. Spring waters swept away anything that wasn't nailed down and a few things that were, no doubt to the amusement of those in Williams Landing. From their chairs on the porches of the Front Street saloons, they watched Leflore's bricks and wood float by on their way to New Orleans. Within a few years, all trace of Point Leflore was gone and Williams Landing was secure.

Apparently, the leaders of Williams Landing were a forgiving bunch; when the town was large enough to be incorporated in 1844, they chose the name "Greenwood." River traffic was steady and building. Cotton was brought from a distance of up to sixty miles to be shipped at Greenwood, and the town boasted 150 citizens by 1850. Twenty businesses had opened their doors and up to 30,000 cotton bales were rolling down the planks from the warehouses onto the boats each year. Over three hundred miles of Delta levees were built in the 1850s, opening up new land for cotton production. The big money of marketing was still confined to Memphis and New Orleans, with Greenwood serving only as a shipping point.

The town itself was still rough around the edges, with saloons on every corner to serve the dock hands and riverboat captains. The Delta was a wilderness and that atmosphere permeated the young town. In 1855, the aldermen were compelled to ask I. N. Welch to "remove his pet bear and put him in some place where he can do no damage to person or property." While hill towns were forming lyceum societies and organizing colleges, Greenwoodians were just intent on surviving day to day without drowning or being eaten by wild beasts.

The Civil War ended Mississippi's first cotton kingdom and slowed Greenwood's river traffic dramatically. The town itself served no strategic advantage for either North or South, but it would be the site of an unusual battle that delayed the capture of Vicksburg. In early 1863, a frustrated U. S. Grant was still looking for a back-door approach to Vicksburg, having been thwarted in his attempt to take it by direct river attack and overland march across Mississippi. Studying a map of the Delta, he devised a plan to dynamite the levee at Moon Lake and move a flotilla of gunboats down the Coldwater River, into the Tallahatchie and then the Yazoo, eventually coming into Vicksburg from the north.

Perhaps in Grant's native Ohio, this would have worked. But in the backwaters of the Mississippi Delta, it turned into a tragicomic nightmare. Confederate soldiers and plantation owners, amazed by the site of this armada struggling down the narrow Coldwater and Tallahatchie rivers, felled giant cottonwoods and sycamores across the channel and then took potshots at Union soldiers who sank to their knees in the thick gumbo trying to wrestle the stumps out of the way. Laboriously, the group of boats made its way into the main channel of the Tallahatchie; Confederate leaders quit laughing and began to get a bit worried. Their ace-in-the-hole was just west of Greenwood, where the Tallahatchie takes a ninety-degree turn to the east to meet the Yalobusha, form the Yazoo, and double back on itself at the elbow turn. Cotton bales and earthworks were piled up here to form a crude fortification, dubbed Fort Pemberton. Similar fortifications were built at the old Point Leflore site. The *Star of the West,* an elegant old sidewheeler which had drawn the first shots in anger at Charleston Harbor in January, 1861, was stripped of its engines at Yazoo City, towed to Greenwood and sunk crosswise in the Tallahatchie's channel.

Early on the morning of March 11, 1863, the Union ironclad *Chillocothe* rounded the sharp turn in the Tallahatchie and slowed when its lookouts spotted the *Star of the West's* superstructure looming ahead. That hesitation was fatal; the cannons of Fort Pemberton opened with all their force and shattered the ship's turret. Four days of repeated attempts yielded the same

On the original street where Williams Landing began, cotton factoring offices overlooked the Yazoo River. Viking Range corporation is refurbishing these buildings for use as their corporate headquarters.

results, and the fleet finally retreated northward to retrace its steps into the Mississippi River. Grant would eventually take Vicksburg, but he wouldn't do it through the Delta.

Reconstruction brought Greenwood into a new county, Leflore, with a new designation as county seat. Boat traffic was building up again slowly and three hundred citizens lived in the town, served by three stores and twice as many saloons. There was no courthouse until 1879; court was held in the Grange Hall. Two hotels were built, the Allen House and the Reiman Hotel, and Greenwood struggled toward respectability.

By 1880, the census had risen by the pitiful count of eight citizens. It would take two massive projects by the recently reviled U. S. government to initiate Greenwood's prosperous days. Congress had authorized a far-reaching levee construction project, draining the swamps of the Delta and revealing topsoil which would grow cotton more efficiently than any other land in the world. All that cotton had to be shipped to market in some manner. Dredgers churned up the channel of the Yazoo, clearing out old wrecks and sunken gunboats. With the river wide open and cotton pouring in, Greenwood was ready to grow. The arrival of the Yazoo and Mississippi Valley Railroad in 1886 was almost incidental. By 1889, Greenwood's prosperity was assured, but it still conveyed the image of a rough river town. Thirteen saloons and twenty-two boarding houses and hotels lined Front Street and Ramcat Alley. Not surprisingly, a local chapter of the Women's Temperance Union was started in 1891; undoubtedly, there were some interesting confrontations along the riverfront over the next few years.

More significant than the temperance ladies in Greenwood's turnaround

C. E. Wright brought Artesian wells and public utilities to Greenwood, and managed to have this house built for his wife, Daisy, without her awareness that it was to be their home.

was the capture of the cotton marketing business locally. Raising cotton had brought many a fortune to the Delta, and shipping it was a profitable enterprise, but the real money was made on the marketing end. To date, that money had stayed in cities like Memphis and New Orleans. In the 1890s, Greenwood's first marketing firms opened and soon Front Street was lined with cotton factors. Mississippi's second cotton kingdom was taking shape and Greenwood would be its capital.

Greenwood was slowly turning into a real town. Its streets had always been a muddy mess, rutted by cotton wagons and horses. Cypress planks laid down in the 1880s helped somewhat, but those were torn up by heavy circus wagons in 1889. Mayor E. L. Miller threatened the show's owners with every manner of legal action, and the reparations paid by the circus paved Greenwood's first hard-surfaced roads.

Streets were a promising start, but many towns across Mississippi were building the infrastructure which would carry them into a modern world of electric lights and public utilities. C. E. Wright had come to Greenwood to begin an ice business, a sure source of income in the Delta's humid summers. He expanded it into Citizens Ice, Coal and Electric Light Company and began to look for new sources of clear water for freezing. Drilling nine hundred feet into the Delta's soft soil, he brought in Greenwood's first Artesian well, one of dozens which would supply the growing needs of the city. Wright would be the driving force behind the modernization of Greenwood, installing the first electric system and water works and then selling them to the city.

Mr. Wright would also build one of Greenwood's most gracious homes, practically in the shadow of Greenwood Utilities' power plant. Soon after he married his wife, Daisy, he began construction of an elegant one-and-a-half-story Queen Anne house with fifteen rooms and a deep wraparound porch. Each day, he drove Daisy by to see this elegant home going up, giving her no

hint that it was to be theirs. When it was finished in 1898, he presented her with the key.

Greenwood was growing every direction but north, hemmed in there by the same Yazoo waters which had given it a reason to exist. Senator J. Z. George's plantation filled the peninsula between the Yazoo and Tallahatchie rivers, accessible only by ferry. In 1894, an iron drawbridge was built and a few houses and stores appeared in the village of "North Greenwood."

The dawn of the twentieth century found Greenwood riding a wave of cotton money and statewide power. The architectural remnants of its early days were destroyed when the Allen House caught fire in April, 1900. The flames consumed most of the old waterfront and much of downtown. Businesses rapidly rebuilt, bigger and better, and public sentiment demanded a new courthouse to replace the modest one built in 1879. It was demolished and R. H. Hunt, the South's premier architect, was hired to design a new one. He bowed to the Beaux Arts mania sweeping the country, giving Leflore County one of the state's most imposing public buildings. Two stories of ashlar stone were topped with a balustraded mansard roof and fronted by a full-height Ionic portico. Towering above the

This monumental structure, the Leflore County Courthouse, is made of ashlar stone and stands on the site where Choctaw Indians conducted their religious rituals. It was built in 1904 and enlarged in 1950.

R. H. Hunt, the South's premier architect, gave Leflore County one of the state's most imposing public buildings.

Yazoo was a three-stage clock tower with four faces.

All too aware that their new buildings could be gone in a careless moment, the citizens of Greenwood formed a fire company in 1906. Mayor Will Vardaman trekked to Memphis to buy two horses and a fire wagon, and Fire Station Number One was built at the south end of Howard Street. Three full-time firemen lived in the red brick station, throwing open the arched doorways onto Carrollton Avenue whenever the alarm bells sounded. In 1913, the city supplemented the horse-drawn water wagon with the latest "automatic fire machine."

Greenwood's population grew from 3,000 in 1900 to 7,000 in 1907. As progressive as the community was, it was not immune to the wave of Civil War nostalgia which was sweeping over Mississippi in the first decades of the century. Every dusty little hamlet had to have a Confederate memorial, traditionally an obelisk topped by a lone sentry. Greenwood's United Daughters of the Confederacy and Confederate Veterans organizations would have none of that. Their monument would be grandiose and heavily populated. With local pledges and a $5,000 appropriation from the Board of Supervisors in hand, they began negotiations with Columbus Marble Works. The memorial would be built of "the best personally selected flawless silver gray Georgia marble" with the statuary "cut out of the best perfect Italian marble, cut in Italy." No less than six figures were ordered, including an artillery man, a cavalryman, a sentry, a "sure-enough woman" (meaning no angelic figures with

In 1915, the United Daughters of the Confederacy dedicated the state's only Confederate Memorial Building in Greenwood. It has since served as a children's clinic, an Air Force Cadet Club, and the site of numerous receptions and garden shows.

outstretched wings) and two figures memorializing Lewis Sharkey Morgan, who had been killed in the battle of Collierville at age fifteen. His niece and great-nephew posed for the statues and orders were sent to Georgia for Kennesaw Mountain stone.

With much ceremony and an estimated six hundred Confederate veterans in attendance, the monument was unveiled and dedicated on October 9, 1913. The indomitable UDC wasn't finished; wheedling yet another $5,000 from the generous county supervisors, they began plans for an entire Confederate Memorial Building, the only one of its kind in the state. Land was donated by Dr. and Mrs. T. R. Henderson; C. E. Wright and other businessmen kicked in $4,500 and the local veterans came up with $500. In 1915, the red brick modified-Gothic building was finished, complete with a large stone porch and battlemented parapet. The names of Civil War veterans were carved in stone tablets flanking the entrances; within a few years, a long list of World War I veterans would be added.

The Hendersons were a wealthy and philanthropic couple, generous with the money which "Miss Lizzie George" had inherited from her father, Senator J. Z. George. When Dr. Henderson died, she had Westminster Chimes installed in the courthouse clock tower as a memorial. A Carnegie Foundation pledge of $10,000 for a library was met by Miss Lizzie's donation of land next to the Confederate Memorial Building for its site. Beautifully designed in a Jacobean Revival style with a multitude of steep gables and chimney stacks, the library was entered through doorways framed by pointed stone arches and fanciful carvings of open books.

While the UDC was memorializing, Cotton Row was bustling, having weathered the setback of the dreaded boll weevils. Front Street, Howard Street and even Ramcat Alley were being bricked, their surfaces covered in intricate patterns by a master mason who worked from dawn until dusk with three assistants. At crosswalks, brass reflectors marked the path for pedestrians.

Greenwood was pushing out in every direction, and those lands across the Yazoo were just begging for development. Captain Sam Gwin, E. R. McShane and W .T. Loggins devised a plan for the old J. Z. George place; they would build a "Grand Boulevard," eighty feet wide with a broad central median, lined with large lots and ten-acre estates. The "Boulevard Subdivision" would be the showplace of Greenwood, running from the drawbridge over the Yazoo to the Tallahatchie River.

Only one obstacle stood in the way of development. A Victorian farmhouse was sitting square in the path of the proposed road. Rather than tearing it down, the owners jacked it up on logs, hooked the frame to mules and had it pulled a few hundred feet to the northeast. They intended for it to be the first house to face the new boulevard, but they must have had their backs turned when the mules stopped pulling. It was set down facing a side street and there it would stay.

While Captain Gwin was moving houses and laying out streets, his wife was hatching a plan which would change the image of Greenwood forever. Sally Humphreys Gwin, known to all as "Miss Sally," was the independent granddaughter of Mississippi's first Reconstruction governor. She envisioned much more than a street linking the two rivers; in her mind, it would be lined with shady oaks for future generations to enjoy. Captain Gwin, wise enough not to argue, assigned her a crew of men headed by Horace Greeley Austin. For weeks, the Gwins rode the Tallahatchie riverbanks and shores of local lakes, choos-

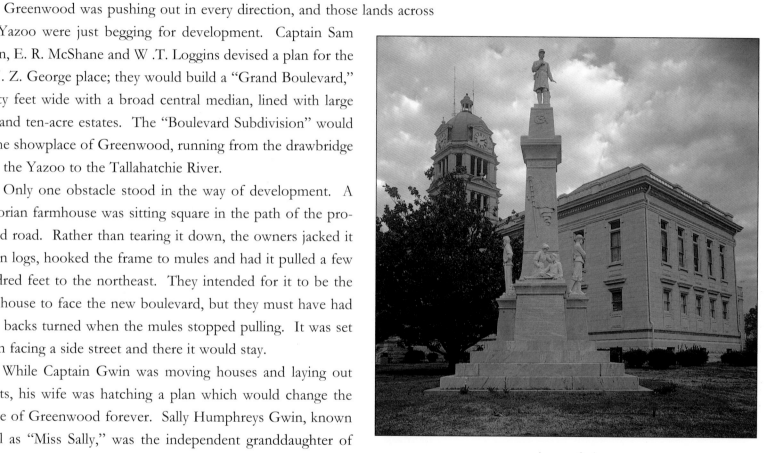

Greenwood's Confederate Monument is unique in the sheer number of statues crowded onto it, boasting six in all. Local citizens posed for the figures and it was unveiled in 1913.

Stretching in an unbroken arch from river to river, the hundreds of trees on Grand Boulevard inspired a New York writer to label it "The Most Beautiful Street in America."

ing pin oak saplings suitable for transplant. Greeley Austin followed behind in a wagon filled with water buckets. Each tree was blazed on its north side, transferred into a bucket and carried back to the boulevard excavation. Miss Sally would march across the Yazoo bridge daily, followed by her five children, and parade down the boulevard marking the exact spots where the trees were to be planted. Through the night, the long-suffering Greeley and his men would plant the young trees. Hundreds were lined up along the mile-long road between the rivers. As the estates were bought up and Neoclassic, Spanish Revival and Tudor homes built, the trees grew. The Gwin house was built on the highest lot on the boulevard, and Miss Sally spent the next forty years admiring the beauty she had originated. Stretching in an unbroken arch from river to river, the trees inspired a New York writer to label this "The Most Beautiful Street in America."

By 1923, Grand Boulevard and its side streets had attracted 1,700 residents and North Greenwood was incorporated into the city proper. Dozens of Model Ts and wagons were making the trip across the rickety iron drawbridge every day, and it was becoming obvious that a more modern bridge would soon be needed. River traffic was a fraction of what it had been fifty years before, but enough boats still came through to make a moveable span of some sort mandatory. The iron bridge was demolished and a temporary wooden piling built. Next to it, Riley-Bailey Construction Company of St.

Louis began to fashion the structure which would come to symbolize Greenwood. Keesler Bridge was nearly three hundred feet long with a soaring steel superstructure above concrete piers. Wooden walkways were lined by cast concrete balustrades covering the machinery which ran underneath the roadway. By May, 1925, it was ready for traffic. A Bridge Queen was chosen, ribbons were stretched across the entrances and most of Greenwood gathered on the riverbanks to watch the marvel of this bridge that turned. The motors were fired up and the span pulled away from the banks, rotating on its central pier in a wide arc until it sat at midstream. When the boats had passed, the process was reversed.

Rivers could provide entertainment and engineering marvels, but they could also turn ugly. The record-breaking Mississippi River Flood of 1927 didn't reach as far east as Greenwood, but thousands of refugees were sheltered there during the weeks following the levee breaks. Greenwoodians were too smug about their immunity to disaster. In 1932, after an unusually rainy winter, the Tallahatchie jumped its banks and came roaring down Grand Boulevard, meeting the Yazoo at Keesler Bridge. Most of the lots along the boule-

Three businessmen envisioned a fashionable subdivision stretching from the Yazoo River to the Tallahatchie River in North Greenwood. "Miss Sally" Gwin made it a landmark by planting a mile of oaks on each side of the road, Grand Boulevard.

vard were built up enough to keep the water from the houses, but those that had basements did find them convenient spots for fishing. For weeks, the boulevard was lost under several feet of brown water. Cars gave way to boats, and the city built a wooden pier the length of the street for homeowners to tie up. Still, it was spring and this was the Delta. Old pictures show fashionably dressed partygoers being hauled through the water on mule drawn wagons, their dresses and high heels tucked carefully into buckets.

When the waters finally receded, levees were built along both banks of the Yazoo, and this city of rivers has seen water in its streets on only a couple of occasions since the Great Flood of 1932. Other things have changed: soybeans and catfish ponds have taken over many of the old cotton fields, and Cotton Row is a quieter corner of town than it used to be. The brick streets are buried under several layers of asphalt, and the Carnegie Library has been empty for many years, replaced by a more modern building of steel and glass across the street.

The Confederate Memorial Building was used as a pediatric clinic and a Cadet Club for the thousands of airmen stationed at Greenwood during World War II. A disastrous fire nearly destroyed the building in 1992, but a concerted effort by the Greenwood Women's Club and the UDC brought it back to life for another generation of piano recitals and garden club shows.

Greenwood still bills itself as "The Cotton Capital of the World," although several of the billboards which carry that boast are surrounded by soybean fields. Cotton lost its dominance with the rise of synthetic fabrics in the post-WWII years and much of the marketing moved to other areas. Several cotton factors still have offices along Front Street and Main, but a few of the old offices are being revitalized for Viking Industries.

The Leflore County Courthouse was enlarged in 1953, with symmetrical wings adding to its enormity. In the 1970s, the entire structure was found to

Mayor Will Vardaman personally travelled to Memphis to select the horses and fire wagon for Fire Station Number One in 1906. The building would later house the American Red Cross.

be slowly sliding toward the Yazoo River, which had cut erosive tunnels beneath its foundation. County offices were moved to the old hospital while a multimillion-dollar stabilization was performed. High up in the clock tower, Lizzie George Henderson's chimes ring out every fifteen minutes. The little crowd of marble statues still stand guard over the southeast corner of the lawn.

Fire Station Number One was replaced by more modern facilities decades ago. Its horses and wagons were retired, and the building was turned into an American Red Cross office. The arched doorway, where Mayor Vardaman's horses once thundered out onto Howard Street with the fire wagon rocking behind them, was long ago enclosed. The station sits empty, its bricks crumbling and the window sills rotting from lack of paint.

Around the corner, C. E. Wright's "Daisy" is still in the family. Greenwood Utilities' sprawling power plant stands fortress-like across the street. The Artesian well which Wright tapped a century ago bubbled for years out of a granite fountain on the grounds of Davis Elementary School. The school burned in 1980, but the fountain remains as a reminder of the man who pulled Greenwood into the twentieth century.

Grand Boulevard's estate houses have aged gracefully, shaded by Miss Sally's giant oaks. Walking the sidewalks of the boulevard is not an adventure for the faint-of-heart; pushed up by the massive roots of those old trees, the concrete rolls and tilts at crazy angles and will trip up an inattentive stroller. In any other location, this might be cause for felling a tree, but not on the boulevard. Those oaks are a sacred trust, coming down only when strong storms twist their roots out of the Delta dirt. Even then, they are hovered over and mourned like lifelong friends.

Capping the south end of the boulevard is the indomitable Keesler Bridge, a beloved anachronism from an age of steamboats and cotton barges.

Most of the traffic now crosses on Hinman Bridge or Veterans Bridge. The concrete piers of Keesler are showing some wear and there's a spot or two in the wooden walkway where the swirling waters of the Yazoo can be seen between the boards. No one seems to know if the turning machinery still works. The last time it was tried, in the early 1950s, the bridge stuck in the open position, leading to quite a bit of civic consternation and more than one missed appointment. With the last of the big boats a distant memory, it really doesn't matter. Keesler Bridge serves a more important function now, as an anchor symbolizing this town which grew from the Yazoo.

Brookhaven

Samuel Moreton
House

Lampton Auditorium serves as the centerpiece of Whitworth College, founded in 1858 by Brookhaven philanthropist Milton Whitworth.

*M*ilton Whitworth must have been a very persuasive man. Within the span of a few years, he convinced a railroad engineer to reroute his tracks, revived a dying college and altered the career of an unsuspecting architect who was just trying to get home to Baltimore. Whitworth's vision and persistence built Brookhaven and Whitworth College and left a mark on this south Mississippi town which is evident today.

In 1850, Whitworth didn't have many neighbors on which to practice his powers of persuasion. The land which would become Brookhaven had been pretty much ignored since its cession from the Choctaw Indians in 1805. A few farmers raised scrubby cotton in the clearings between the thick pine forests and a herd or two of cattle grazed in the valleys. The land was hilly and cheap, going for 12½ cents an acre on a good day.

Samuel Jayne had found his way here from Long Island, New York, in 1818. He amassed a fair amount of land and built a sawmill and store in the village he dubbed "Brookhaven." Jayne was apparently lacking in ambition or desire for company; when the New Orleans, Jackson and Great Northern Railroad surveyors came by looking for routes, he shooed them off his land. He wanted no part of the iron rails tracing their way across Mississippi.

Jayne's neighbor to the west, Milton Whitworth, was a different sort. He owned a considerable plantation and saw the potential for growth of the area if the railroad came through. Ezekiel Hudnall owned 320 acres adjacent to Whitworth's land; Whitworth offered him $1000 if he would make that land available for the railroad right-of-way. Hudnall saw a fat profit looming for the $40 he had invested in the acreage, and he readily agreed to Whitworth's scheme. Whitworth then collared George Hazlehurst, chief engineer of the New Orleans line, and offered him a free right-of-way under one condition: every passenger train that came through the new town had to stop. Hazlehurst agreed and directed his surveyors from Jayne's property onto Hudnall's.

Most everyone but Jayne packed up and left the old Brookhaven for the new one. The first train steamed into town in March, 1858, preceded by a flatcar with a cannon that boomed out at every whistlestop. Milton Whitworth was delighted. He already had great plans for his new town and the wherewithal to make those plans a reality. Certain that new stores and houses would follow the railroad, he opened a sawmill and installed the state's first circular saw in it. A real town needed churches, so Whitworth gave the land and lumber to build First Methodist Church.

Churches and sawmills were a start, but Brookhaven was a relative latecomer in Mississippi's cultural circles and had a lot of catching up to do. In antebellum Mississippi, every respectable community had a college, and Whitworth was determined that Brookhaven would acquire one immediately. It would be difficult to start from scratch, but he knew of a slightly used institution that had fallen on hard times. Elizabeth Female Academy, founded in 1818 in Washington as the distaff equivalent to Jefferson Military College, had dwindled to nothing after an 1840s fire. Officially, it was still chartered under the auspices of the Mississippi Methodist Conference; all Whitworth had to do was talk the Methodist leaders into transferring the school to Brookhaven.

Long abandoned, Whitworth College's historic structures are being renovated to house the Mississippi School for Fine Arts.

In the few hours it took for the train to steam between New Orleans and Brookhaven, Baltimore architect Alfred Moreton's ticket home had been canceled and he had a new job building a college he had never heard of in a town where he had never been. He never left.

Once again, Whitworth poured on the charm and doled out the money. Elizabeth Female Academy was formally moved to Brookhaven and reopened as Whitworth College. It existed on paper only; buildings would be needed as soon as possible. Mississippi's slim cadre of architects and professional builders had their hands full with the last of the pre-war Greek Revival and Italianate mansions going up around the state, and Whitworth was desperate for someone who could put together his campus.

Fate stepped in on a train trip. Whitworth was returning from a New Orleans visit when he chanced to meet young Alfred E. Moreton. Moreton was a Baltimore architect who had been in Louisiana consulting on the French Opera House. He was returning home when Whitworth waylaid him. In the few hours it took for the train to steam between New Orleans and Brookhaven, Moreton's ticket home had been canceled and he had a new

Recruited by Milton Whitworth to design the campus of Whitworth College, A. E. Moreton left a lasting impression on the architecture of Brookhaven. He built this house for his new bride.

Brookhaven exists because Milton Whitworth persuaded the railroad to change course and bring every passenger train from Jackson to New Orleans to the depot.

job, building a college he had never heard of in a town where he had never been. He never left.

Inspired by Whitworth's enthusiasm and deep pockets, Moreton hit the ground running. Classroom and dormitory buildings went up and by 1859 Whitworth was ready to admit its first class. It was an auspicious start in an inauspicious time. Only two groups of graduates would finish the curriculum before the Civil War closed Whitworth's doors. The buildings were converted into a Confederate hospital, and it was as a medical center that Brookhaven rode out the war. Its railroad lines were destroyed, but the full fury of war never reached the fledgling town. Dozens of wounded soldiers were brought in from battles around the state; those that died were temporarily buried on the lawns of Whitworth College.

When the war ended, it was time to get Brookhaven back on track again, literally and figuratively. The burned and twisted rail ties were replaced and once again the trains stopped at Brookhaven's depot. Milton Whitworth continued to pour money into his college, readying it for an anticipated post-war enrollment boom. Alfred Moreton was working on his own new home for his bride, Laura Decell, but he was also busy trying to keep up with Whitworth's building plans. In just a few years, the campus added Margaret Hall, a domed Greek Revival classroom building, along with Johnson Institute and the Brown House.

One of the first instructors at Whitworth, Mrs. Annie Paten, was an alumnae of the school. She was an early proponent of higher education for women, and jumped on the bandwagon when the state appropriated funds for a women's public college. Whitworth College would be a logical choice, she argued. It was well-located, full of brand-new buildings and blessed with an outstanding faculty. Unfortunately for her crusade, Methodist Bishop Charles Galloway disagreed. He blocked the deal with the state and the charter went to Columbus Female Institute, which would grow into Mississippi University for Women.

When Milton Whitworth died in 1870, his dreams of a town and a college had been realized. His civic banner was picked up by his protegé, Alfred Moreton. Since that fateful train ride from New Orleans, Moreton had cut his ties to the North, even serving in the Confederate army. With the campus of Whitworth temporarily finished, he turned his building skills to downtown Brookhaven. He designed the first brick building in town, and, in 1880, he was one of the first to catch the lumbering fever sweeping the Piney Woods region. Brookhaven was surrounded by towering pine forests; as the railroads penetrated deeper into the region, lumbering became big business. Moreton joined forces with another northern expatriate, Captain J. J. Helms, to form Moreton and Helms Lumber Company, south Mississippi's first large mill. Before the giant operations in Hattiesburg, Laurel and Meridian had even gotten started, Brookhaven was shipping out railcars full of pine boards for America's building boom.

Through the remainder of the nineteenth century, Moreton's lumber business grew along with Brookhaven. In 1899, he sold Moreton and Helms and organized the Pearl River Lumber Company in Pearlhaven. Fully automated, it grew into the largest lumber operation in the state. Each Monday, the notoriously frugal Moreton would walk the ten miles to the Pearlhaven plant and spend the week there, walking back home on Friday. The first phone lines installed in Brookhaven connected his office with his home.

In the heyday of the railroads, the conveniently located Inez Hotel was the center of Brookhaven's social whirl.

Brookhaven at the turn of the century was booming, having survived civic dissension in the 1890s when the state actually took control of the city government. Whitworth College was one of the state's premier educational institutions. One of its administrators went on to head Millsaps College; another founded Belhaven College. Under the leadership of Dr. I. W. Cooper, Whitworth launched its most ambitious building spree. Between 1904 and 1920, six new buildings redefined the old campus. Enochs Hall, Cooper Hall, a gymnasium with an indoor swimming pool and a new President's Home were all built in this period.

The crowning glory of the campus was Lampton Auditorium. Funded partially by the five sons of Mary Jane Lampton, it was built in 1915 in the popular Neoclassic style. A recessed colonnade supported by monumental Ionic columns opened into the 800-seat auditorium. Music Department chairman Elizabeth McVoy lured in artists and performers from around the country, transforming Lampton into the cultural center of south Mississippi.

Downtown Brookhaven was also growing and bustling with the arrival of eighteen passenger trains daily on several lines. In November, 1907, the new Union Depot opened, its red tile roof and elaborate brick-paved walkways the first sight which many visitors had of Brookhaven. Nearby was the Romanesque Revival Inez Hotel, named by owners Mr. and Mrs. R. T. Scherck in honor of their daughter. For decades, its spacious lobby and restaurant were the center of social life in Brookhaven.

While the city and college were being reshaped, Alfred Moreton was scaling back from the lumber business to putter in his workshop. Brookhaven had a large and prosperous Jewish community, and many of them were friends of Moreton. When they died, he would labor in his workshop to craft the pegged coffins which their beliefs required. Moreton was also single-handedly populating South Jackson Avenue. His own home had stood there

$\mathcal{O}$nly one town in Mississippi nearly lost its status as county seat because of its reputation as a rowdy, ill-mannered nest of lowlifes. It wasn't Natchez, with its "Under-the-Hill" keelboaters fighting in the streets, or Biloxi, haven for pirates and gamblers. Nor was it the rough-and-tumble lumber camps that grew into Hattiesburg and Laurel.

The town with the terrible reputation was Tupelo. During its first thirty years, respectable merchants and townspeople despaired of ever gaining the upper hand in their war with the baser elements of society. When the Lee County Courthouse burned in 1873, neighboring towns lobbied hard to have their government affairs moved away from Tupelo and into the more sedate environs of Saltillo or Verona. Fortunately for Tupelo, they were unsuccessful.

Tupelo's story begins in 1832, almost forty years before it was incorporated as a town. The Treaty of Pontotoc brought thousands of settlers into north Mississippi, eager to buy up Chickasaw lands for little more than a dollar per acre. Most rode right past the hills bordering Town Creek, bound for the boom towns of Holly Springs and Oxford and Pontotoc. The area that would become Tupelo was bought up by speculators like Christopher Orr, William Harris and George Thomason. Maybe someday it would be worth something, but for their own homesteads they chose sites closer to the Natchez Trace in Pontotoc County. Orr's hamlet of Palmetto never amounted to more than a few small houses, but Harrisburg actually expanded to include a post office, three stores, a Methodist church and a Masonic Lodge by 1851.

Transportation was a crucial element in antebellum Mississippi; a town without a navigable river or a decent road would never draw any business. A trip to the nearest store over rutted cowpaths could be a long, dangerous journey. By the mid-1850s, change was coming, and it came with the sound of iron spikes being hammered into railroad ties. Entire towns like Vaiden and Brookhaven moved en masse to intersect with the railroad.

Tupelo's start would lead to the extinction of Harrisburg. Orr, Harris and Thomason discovered that the Mobile and Ohio Railroad surveyors were marking their lines several miles east of Harrisburg. Being canny land speculators, they knew that whoever owned the land where those tracks passed would likely make a nice profit. They cleared title to a large block of land straddling the proposed rail line and platted off sixty-two lots. This empty spot would be called "Tupelo," a Chickasaw word for "place of lodging." Nothing about the site differentiated it from any other farmland in north Mississippi; Town Creek was navigable at times, but just as often was a shallow, muddy ditch. No rich Delta topsoil lured planters eager to grow cotton; this was just a hilly corner of the Black Belt with some scattered hardwood forests. But the great Iron Horses that spelled progress were moving closer every day, and Tupelo's sixty-two lots were quickly snapped up in 1860.

Most of Harrisburg migrated east to the new town. It was nothing more than a ramshackle collection of saloons, boarding houses and brothels, thrown together overnight to grab the railroad workers' paychecks. Front Street ran parallel to the tracks, and it was a twenty-four-hour-a-day circus. Harrisburg immigrants built their houses west of the tracks and wondered what kind of a town they had chosen.

The Civil War began before Tupelo was even a year old; most of the landowners in the area were small farmers with no slaves, but they dutifully marched off to war. Railroad traffic trickled to a halt and Tupelo stagnated.

Reconstruction found Tupelo in a newly created county defiantly named for Robert E. Lee.

A major confrontation at the old Harrisburg site brought the war right to Tupelo's doorstep. As Union forces won control of Mississippi, hundreds of miles of tracks were destroyed, and the future of this tiny railroad-dependent hamlet looked increasingly dim.

Reconstruction found Tupelo in a newly-created county, formed from parts of Pontotoc and Itawamba counties and defiantly named for Robert E. Lee. The first county seat was awarded to Saltillo, but that town was too far north to suit southern Lee countians. In 1867, the seat of government was moved to Tupelo. Tupelo was rebuilding after the war, but once again the baser elements were in control. Front Street was still lined with all manner of questionable businesses. Horsemen too lazy to dismount rode right into businesses and church services were interrupted by roaming bands of pigs and dogs. A few finer houses were being built along North Broadway, but even those fought for space with saloons. Major Henry Clay Medford, the first mayor of Tupelo when it was belatedly incorporated in 1870, could look out of his parlor window on North Broadway and see right into the saloon across the street. Next door to that bar, conveniently enough, was the jail and jailer's

In Tupelo's chaotic early years, this block of North Broadway Street housed several saloons, the jail and the jailer's house.

If one railroad could create a town out of nothing, surely two would be the key to prosperity. Once again, the sound of railroad construction echoed through Lee County.

house. Derelicts who couldn't quite make it home could simply collapse on the jailhouse porch and wait for the jailer to unlock the door. Mayor Medford's opinion on the neighborhood activity was not preserved for posterity.

A small courthouse was built on the square in 1871. It burned rather mysteriously in 1873, with all county records salvaged. Controversy instantly arose over where to locate the new courthouse. Citizens of nearby Verona were tired of dodging drunks and street fighters when they ventured into Tupelo on government business; they campaigned vigorously for a removal of the county seat to their town, an oasis of respectability compared to Tupelo. Mayor Medford and the more stable of his 618 fellow Tupeloans won the day, and the new brick courthouse remained on the square.

As Mississippi recovered from war and Reconstruction, the hilly farm-land around Tupelo was starting to fill with new settlers. They needed a commercial center, and a small spark of civic pride began to flare in Tupelo. Legitimate businesses grew up along Main Street, insulating their storefronts from the embarrassment of Front Street by designating the intervening blocks as "parking lots." Farmers could hitch their wagons and buggies there and go directly to shop on Main Street.

Tupelo was at a crossroads, teetering between a rough village and a bustling commercial center. In a tradition which would repeat itself again and again over the next century, civic leaders emerged to guide the direction of the town. *Tupelo Daily Journal* owner John Miller was the first of a long line of crusading editors to head the newspaper; "Private" John Allen was just beginning a seventeen-year career in the U. S. House of Representatives. These two men began a campaign to bring the Kansas City, Memphis and Birmingham Railroad through Tupelo. If one railroad could create a town out of nothing, surely two would be the key to prosperity. Neighboring Verona was still smarting over its loss in the county seat selection and was agitating for a railroad of its own. When Miller and Allen promised to name a major thoroughfare for Captain Gloster, chief engineer of the K C, M & B, the battle was won. Once again, the sound of railroad construction echoed through Lee County, and in 1886 John Allen drove the final spike of the new line just south of town.

The railroads cemented Tupelo's future, but its direction was given an immeasurable boost when fire wiped out most of Front Street in the late 1880s. The citizens of Tupelo said "Never again." Fifty new brick buildings were built within a year, establishing downtown as a major commercial center, and local prohibition was passed just in case anyone was thinking of rebuilding Front Street.

Tupelo was entering its first years of real prosperity. The old saloon and jail on North Broadway were gone, replaced by attractive Queen Anne and Gothic Revival homes. The first public school was built in Freeman's Grove and oil-burning street lights lit the night skies. To be a true city in the 1890s, an opera house was a must, and Tupelo built one with the state's largest stage and nine hundred seats.

Cotton was the fuel for Lee County's agricultural engine, but it was rivaled in the early 1890s by a fledgling pulpwood industry. A planing mill was built and several factories grew up to utilize the lumber production in turning out chairs, wheel spokes and tool handles.

Tupelo High School sent out its first graduates in 1894. They were headed into a local job market which seemed robust, but was actually headed for a fall. Forty years of cotton farming had depleted the thin Black Belt topsoil, and the plunge in cotton prices to five cents a pound put many farmers out of business. The pulpwood industry also failed, shutting down the small factories which depended on it for material. As the nineteenth century gave way to the twentieth, Tupelo was in the financial doldrums with no foreseeable economic miracle on the horizon. For the first time in its history, more people were leaving Lee County than were moving in, and even the pride of Tupelo, its magnificent Opera House, had to close its doors.

Private John Allen was not about to let his hometown dwindle and die. Cobbling together a group of local businessmen and $220,000, he oversaw the creation of Tupelo Cotton Mill. Its purpose was to provide jobs for desperate farm families and offer a local market for the area's cotton production. Situated close to the intersection of the two railroads, the huge mill opened in 1901 with 170 looms and 500 spindles. Its four-story brick water tower loomed like a castle battlement over Tupelo. Each day, four hundred and fifty workers turned out twenty-five miles of cotton twill "Tupelo Cheviot." They lived in a mill village constructed especially for them, complete with a school, church, baseball fields and recreation halls. The workers' children were required to attend school and the mill owners took pride in hiring no one under the age of sixteen.

Congressman Allen had used his economic resources to build Tupelo's first major industry; he would use his political clout to bring a national fish

In 1901, Private John Allen and a group of local businessmen combined their resources to open one of Mississippi's largest and most socially progressive cotton mills, complete with housing, schools, churches and recreational facilities.

hatchery to the area. Renowned for his good nature and wit, Allen earned his place in Washington lore with his famous 1901 speech in the House of Representatives, extolling the virtues of Tupelo:

Tupelo is the Center of the Universe. Why, sir, fish will travel overland for miles to get into the water we have in Tupelo. Thousands and millions of unborn fish are clamoring to this Congress today for an opportunity to be hatched at the Tupelo Fish Hatchery.

Persuaded as much by his personality as by his logic, Congress did award the hatchery to Tupelo. Part of the funding provided for an elegant Superintendent's House, built in the popular Queen Anne style with a tower, corbelled chimneys and a shady wraparound porch. It would be the site of numerous weddings, picnics and civic gatherings over the next century.

The Lee County Courthouse, center of so much controversy in 1875, burned in 1902. When the rubble was cleared away and it came time to rebuild, there was no question now but that it would go up on the square in Tupelo. Approximately $86,000 went into the Beaux Arts replacement, fronted at all four entrances by stone columns and topped with a tin roof and clock tower. A block away, the Confederate Monument was dedicated, for some inexplicable reason, in the middle of Main Street. Its base was surrounded by a glass-enclosed goldfish pond, leading to some interesting traffic accidents before it was finally moved to the courthouse lawn in 1934.

The year 1909 ushered in Mayor D. W. Robins' administration, a twenty-year tenure which would see Tupelo surge ahead of its Mississippi neighbors in civic improvements. Robins realized that the town was dependent on its rural customers for its economic base; if they couldn't get to town, they couldn't spend money in Tupelo's stores. And when they got to town, they

When the first Lee County Courthouse burned in 1873, a major campaign developed to move the county seat out of "unsuitable" Tupelo. The current courthouse was finished in 1904.

didn't want to be driving down dusty, rutted paths. Robins pushed through a program of gravelling all roads within three miles of Tupelo's city limits and hard-surfacing the city streets. Granitoid sidewalks were poured along Main Street and other business thoroughfares. The predicted customers came.

One of those newly improved streets led into the fairgrounds of the Mississippi-Alabama Fair and Dairy Show. Dairying had become big business in north Mississippi, promoted as a means of diversification by banker S. J. High. He encouraged his customers, both urban and rural, to be self-supporting with "A cow, a sow, a hen and a factory on every farm." His father-in-law, the ever-resourceful Private John Allen, led the way with an entire herd of Jersey cows happily grazing behind his downtown home. As the dairy industry expanded, a group of promoters bought land east of the railroad tracks and sold stock to establish a fair. An $1,800 grandstand was built, along with a $2,200 racetrack. Children could enter for 25 cents, their parents for 50 cents; they could see displays of farm implements, ride the thrill rides and compete for trinkets. From 1915 until 1917, they could also join hundreds of college students brought in by train for the annual Ole Miss-Mississippi A&M football game. Ole Miss did not thrive in Tupelo; they lost all three games by a combined score of 145-14, including a 65-0 drubbing in 1915 which still stands as their worst loss ever. A near-riot was broken up by both teams' coaches during that game; tempers had flared when A&M's bulldog took a bite out of Ole Miss' goat.

In the years leading up to World War I, Tupelo solidly established its place as the most progressive city in northeast Mississippi. Lumberman R. F. Goodlett felt strongly that such a world-class town could not long be without a theatre, as Tupelo had been since the demise of the Tupelo Opera House. Goodlett donated land next to his Tudor mansion on North Broadway for a new theatre, and the Comus was opened in 1912. Live plays and vaudeville

Built around 1912 as a replacement for the old Opera House, the Lyric Theatre would be transformed from a vaudeville stage to a movie theatre to a community playhouse. It would even serve as a hospital and morgue on the darkest night in Tupelo's history.

gave way to silent movies, and the structure survived at least two fires in 1919 and 1922. Just a few years later, as the Lyric Theatre, it would serve a more serious purpose during Tupelo's darkest hours.

Twenty years after it was built, Tupelo Cotton Mill was running full-blast. Its $4,000 weekly payroll supported 350 workers, turning out 10,000,000 yards of cloth yearly. Forty percent of that production went to the neighboring Tupelo Garment Company, which expanded to 2,500 sewing machines as the 1920s led into the Great Depression.

No one in the cotton mill or garment factory was making a fortune, but they did have the mill village and its social structure to lean on. Farmers were not so fortunate; the Depression was the last blow for many who had been barely eking out a living for years, often without even the luxury of electricity to heat and light their homes. John Rankin had taken the late John Allen's seat in Congress, and he used his close connections to President Roosevelt to put Tupelo in the forefront for power generated by the newly-created Tennessee Valley Authority. The great river was dammed and lines strung from its huge turbines across the Mississippi countryside and into Tupelo, bringing affordable electricity into many homes for the first time. President and Mrs. Roosevelt travelled to Tupelo in 1934 to celebrate this bright spot in the depths of the Depression, and they were greeted by 75,000 enthusiastic supporters packed into the football stadium behind Church Street Primary School.

Tupelo was on a roll, as much as any town could be in the 1930s. Its dubious origins along Front Street were all but forgotten and its tree-lined

In the aftermath of the 1936 tornado, which seriously damaged or destroyed all of Tupelo's schools, parents opted for a reinforced concrete replacement, paid for by WPA funds. This detail from the Church Street School is an example of its bas relief carvings depicting early settlers and Chickasaw Indians.

streets were filled with Victorian and Colonial Revival homes. Tupelo High School had been enlarged in 1927 and its graduates could generally find jobs in one of the industries built with a rare sense of community cohesiveness. In April, 1936, some saw hopeful signs that the worst of America's Depression would soon be over, and Tupeloans felt themselves to be ideally situated to ride new waves of prosperity. All of that changed on the wild night of April 5th.

By all accounts, that Sunday was an odd day. The air was heavy and filled with an ill-defined foreboding. Clouds were building in the west, and a general sense of uneasiness led several pastors to abbreviate their sermons and send their congregations home a little early that evening. Most folks were just starting their bedtime rituals when the wind picked up dramatically. Southwest of town, a thunderhead of unprecedented size dropped an enormous funnel cloud onto the ground, one which would roar through the heart of Tupelo and leave it all but destroyed. In a matter of minutes, entire blocks of homes disappeared. Hundred-year-old trees snapped like matchsticks and were thrown through brick walls like spears. Dozens of people were blown into Gum Pond, and the huge stone pillars of First Baptist Church caved inward as if made of sand. Church Street Primary School vanished altogether; a few blocks away, Tupelo High School was in ruins. Following the devastating winds, torrential rains drenched stunned survivors as they stumbled out into a world turned upside down.

Morning found over 200 people dead in Tupelo. The little hospital on Main Street was in shambles. The city power plant had been shut down to prevent electrocutions, and the Lyric Theatre was pressed into service with its coal-powered generator. The screen was pulled down and the stage turned into a makeshift operating room. Chairs on the left side of the auditorium held the injured and recovering; those on the right side were overlaid with planks and turned into a morgue. Help poured in from across Mississippi;

empty boxcars were loaded with patients and taken to Memphis. It would take days or weeks for some families to locate missing members.

Years would pass before Tupelo completely recovered from one of the deadliest storms in American history. Within days, though, in a show of determination and hope, oak saplings were planted along the littered streets to replace those lost in the storm. Entire families would make their homes in "boxcar cities" while their houses were being rebuilt, and some never learned the fate of relatives who were carried away by the tornado. Tupelo High School was rebuilt in the fashionable Art Deco mode and Church Street School rose from the ruins of the old Primary School. Tupeloans, who for years kept a wary eye on the sky whenever the wind picked up, wanted their children in the safest possible environment. With an awareness of those psychological needs, N. W. Overstreet and Hays Town designed Church Street School as an imposing pink concrete monolith which would withstand anything nature could throw at it. To add a light touch to the curves and round windows of the Art Deco building, bas relief carvings depicted Tupelo's early settlers and Chickasaw Indians.

But 1937 brought another blow to Tupelo, this one economic. After almost four decades of success, Tupelo Cotton Mill was hit with a strike. The mill workers were unhappy with pay and hours, and they closed the plant with a sit-down demonstration. The owners decided to shut the operation down permanently, throwing hundreds out of work. The mill never opened again; the village houses were sold to landlords and many of the workers sadly left the homes where they had grown up. The mill school was closed and its students absorbed into the Tupelo city schools.

Shortly before the outbreak of World War II, a group of businessmen

Elvis Presley spent fall afternoons as a child slipping under the gates of the Mississippi-Alabama Fair and Dairy Show. He would return to Tupelo in 1956 and 1957 for performances at the same fairgrounds, drawing record crowds and donating his fee back to the city.

*A*s Mississippi cities go, Meridian was a late starter. There was just enough of a town there in 1864 for General Sherman to wipe it off the map; riots and financial reverses and epidemics throughout the 1870s squelched any civic optimism. Then the railroads came and for forty years, all roads led to Meridian. If a fledgling community had one railroad in the late 1800s, its success was assured. If it had two, all the better. But if there were five sets of tracks intersecting, as was the case in Meridian, the hotels and stores and public buildings just couldn't be built fast enough to keep up with the boom. By 1907, Mississippi's "Queen City" was welcoming 40 passenger trains daily. Union Station stretched for three blocks through the heart of downtown.

Some of the passengers stepping off those trains were famous faces, bound for performances at Meridian's pride and joy, the Grand Opera House. Towns throughout the state had "opera houses," often little more than a plywood stage and a handful of scratchy horsehair seats. The Grand lived up to its name in every respect. Since its opening in December, 1890, it had hosted the brightest stars of Broadway and the Metropolitan Opera, becoming a favorite stopover on the Atlanta-New Orleans circuit. Theatre goers climbed a wide marble stair to a dark-paneled lobby, supported by square columns imbedded with full-length mirrors. In the auditorium, tiers of gilded balconies curved along the walls and luxurious private boxes bracketed the soaring proscenium arch. High above, an enormous chandelier hung from a sunburst medallion, surrounded by painted stars on a dark blue ceiling.

This was not plantation country; small farmers were the rule, scratching out a living on modest farms planted in cotton and row crops.

From 1890 until 1920, Meridian thrived and the Grand Opera House was its showplace. Opera and live plays gave way to vaudeville. Trees from the pine forests of central Mississippi rumbled through town, piled high on a seemingly endless stream of freight cars. Passenger trains lined up to unload at Union Station. Meridian leapfrogged over Vicksburg to claim the title of Mississippi's largest city. But those three decades were the zenith, and both the city and the Grand Opera House were headed for harder times. The forests thinned out, highways replaced rail travel, and by the late 1920s, Meridian was losing its dominant place in the state's economy. At the Grand, a small screen was hung on the stage in a desperate attempt to hold the crowds who were turning to D. W. Griffith and Charlie Chaplin for entertainment. When the Temple Theatre opened just a few blocks away, the Grand went dark. Safety inspections were failed, the stairs were torn out, and the ground-level lobby was turned into retail space. Walled up, the Grand Opera House quietly vanished from sight, a moldy relic banished to the memory of fewer and fewer Meridianites.

Meridian's rise and fall had been compressed into a remarkably brief period of time. Lauderdale County's land came from the Treaty of Dancing Rabbit Creek in 1830, but settlement there was sparse before the Civil War. This was not plantation country; small farmers were the rule, scratching out a living on modest farms planted in cotton and row crops. One of the larger landowners was Richard McLemore, a Virginian who bought several hundred acres south of Marion, the county seat. Railroads were heading east across Mississippi toward Alabama, and McLemore was well aware that those rails would have to come across someone's land, guaranteeing a profit. Marion seemed to be the likely spot, so he sold his holdings in the country and moved there. Part of his old land went to his daughter, Juriah, and her husband, W. H. Jackson. They built a modest three-room house on the property. The rest of McLemore's holdings were sold to Lewis Ragsdale, an Alabama lawyer, and John T. Ball, a merchant from neighboring Kemper County. Richard McLemore settled in Marion, counting his money and waiting for the railroad.

Good things don't always come to those who just wait. Marion had competition for the Alabama and Vicksburg Railroad. Lewis Ragsdale and John Ball also saw the advantage of land on the rails and they set about building a rival town. From the start, cooperation was not their forte. Bickering and feuding from day one, they fought over the name of the new town and the street designations. What was Ragsdale City to some was Meridian or Showashee Station to others. Street signs went up, only to be pulled down by the rival camp. Engineers of the Alabama and Vicksburg wanted to bypass them altogether, laying rails through Enterprise, but that town brushed them off. Ragsdale, realizing that the chaos in their village was counterproductive, offered unlimited land to the A&V, winning the coveted prize for Ragsdale City/Meridian/Showashee. The Mobile and Ohio was also headed this way, and its line would cross the A&V in the new town.

Two railroads would have been a fortuitous start for any town at any time except 1860. Officially christened "Meridian" in February of that year, this crossroads was little more than a cluster of ramshackle stores, a mill, two churches and a handful of houses, welcoming the first trains of the Alabama and Vicksburg line in May of 1861. These railroads would one day boost Meridian to the top of the state's economic pinnacle, but in wartime, they

The original Union Station was demolished several decades ago. Meridian now boasts a faithful reproduction in its multimodal transportation center.

made it an unwelcome target. The tiny town became a Confederate center, with millions of dollars in equipment and munitions stored here. An arsenal, POW camp and small hospital were added. Meridian was a hub of activity, but it was also squarely in the sights of Union guns.

Vicksburg fell in July, 1863; Jackson was soon under Union control as well. The state government fled, making Meridian the capital for a few days before scuttling upstate to Macon. General Leonidas Polk was in charge of defending what was left of the Confederate munitions and equipment between Meridian and Mobile; he set up headquarters in Juriah Jackson's small house. Word came that General Sherman and ten thousand Union troops were marching east from Jackson. Polk saw no option but evacuation of Meridian, pulling his trains and soldiers into the safety of Alabama. Sherman arrived on Valentine's Day, 1864, to find the prized Confederate supplies gone. His officers divided the available houses among themselves and turned their men loose on the town. Sherman's report summed up their accomplishments:

For five days 10,000 men worked hard and with a will in that work of destruction, with axes, crowbars, sledges, clawbars, and with fire, and I have no hesitation in pronouncing the work as well done. Meridian with its depots, storehouses, arsenal, hospitals, offices, hotels and cantonments no longer exists.

The Jackson house was one of only four or five homes to survive Union occupation. Meridian would have to start from scratch, struggling back to respectability under the burden of Reconstruction. The twisted and burned tracks were rebuilt, and as the trains began to run again, they seemed to be filled with inordinate numbers of carpetbaggers. Tensions ran high in Meridian throughout Reconstruction, especially after it was designated the new county seat in 1870. A full-scale race riot broke out in 1871, leaving dozens dead and relations frayed. The carpetbag mayor fled into the night,

America's postwar building boom was in full swing and thick pine forests of east Mississippi were fueling sawmills all over the area.

never to be seen again, and the city grew fitfully, hobbled by government upheaval, financial panics and a devastating yellow fever epidemic in 1878.

In its first twenty years, Meridian had not seen many good days. But it did have the all-important railroads, and the 1880s brought several other lines through east Mississippi. Cotton was a profitable crop again; even more significant in the long term were the virgin pine forests of east and south Mississippi. America's postwar building boom was in full swing and these thick stands of pines were fueling sawmills all over the area. Meridian lawyer W. H. Hardy pulled together a rail line from Meridian to New Orleans, founding Hattiesburg in the process. Sam Neville developed the Memphis & Meridian line ("Mud and Misery" to those who had to slog through the forests of north Mississippi to build it) and by 1885, five sets of tracks crossed in Meridian. In this boom period, one line was enough to insure economic growth; five meant great things were in store. Within a few years, Front Street was alive with railroad shops, their steam engines and machinery employing five thousand workers. Hotels followed the growing passenger traffic, along with restaurants, saloons and merchants.

Meridian's prosperity was soon reflected in its architecture. The wraparound porches and turrets of Queen Anne homes lined the streets, and older homes were remodeled to reflect current fashion. The old Jackson house had disappeared within the walls of multiple additions, and it grew even larger when businessman J. C. Lloyd moved in. Lloyd owned property in the Market

Mississippi's most opulent 1890s opera house is still hidden behind the storefronts of the Marks-Rothenberg Building. For thirty years, the Grand Opera House attracted the brightest stars of the American stage; in 1927 it fell victim to changing tastes and was sealed up for six decades.

Square section of downtown, rapidly becoming the preferred neighborhood for upscale merchants. He sold a half-block of that property to Isaac Marks, one of a large group of Jewish businessmen who would remake the face of Meridian over the next half-century. Marks and his three half-brothers, Levi, Sam and Marx Rothenberg, had plans to build a massive five-story department store, Meridian's finest by far. This "megabuilding" would house a mercantile complex, hotel, restaurants and an interior courtyard covered with a one-hundred-foot-high glass ceiling. C. M. Rubush, a noted local architect, oversaw construction, and the huge building with monumental rounded archway entrances and an octagonal corner tower began to rise on the corner of 22nd Avenue and Fifth Street.

At some point during construction, plans for a hotel were scrapped and that space was instead devoted to a Grand Opera House. J. B. McElfratrick, designer of opera house interiors for many of America's largest cities, was brought from St. Louis to transform the space into one of the South's most impressive theatres. His $20,000 budget generated a masterpiece, comparable to the great showplaces of Atlanta, New Orleans and Seattle. Opening night, December 17, 1890, found hundreds of Meridian's social elite, dressed to the nines, leaving their carriages along Fifth Street. A reporter from Mobile described the opening night scene:

> *The Opera House. . . . is an oblong building, divided into two nearly equal parts by a proscenium arch. . . . The stage has a thirty-foot opening facing the auditorium and is fifty feet deep. . . . A wide central staircase led to the parquet level lobby. From there, separate staircases led to the dress circle and gallery levels. . . . The parquet is, as in the Mobile Theatre, the fashionable portion of the house, although the dress circle is perhaps the most desirable from which to view the stage performances. The auditorium is illuminated by a sun light in the center of the ceiling, and by bracket lights under the several galleries.*

The interior is decorated throughout in cream, blue, gold and red, but the prevailing tint is gold. The proscenium arch is a heavy frame of gilded work, pierced on either side by the openings for private boxes. . . . There are no angles in the interior of the hall, and the best acoustic effect is obtained. . . . The lobby is spacious, and is approached from the street by a wide staircase. . . . The gallery is reached by a stairway from a side street . . . the interior arrangements are all excellent, everything having been especially arranged to conduce to the comfort and convenience of the patrons.

The stage was backed by twenty-five sets of hand-painted scenery, manufactured by Sossman and Landes Company of Chicago. Dressing rooms lined the backstage walls, heated by steam radiators except for the corner room, outfitted with its own coal-burning fireplace and reserved for the "star" of the day. Narrow speaking tubes carried the director's instructions to stagehands on the catwalks, and tall arched steel doors opened to a cavernous storage room for props and backdrops.

Victorian dandies and ladies could admire their dress in full-length mirrors strategically placed in the square wooden columns of the lobby. Darkwood counters with glass insets held flowers and candy; wise gentlemen purchased their gift, before the show, and ushers would bring the night's surprises down the aisles at intermission.

The Marks-Rothenberg Store and its Opera House were an instant success. Some of its proceeds supported the Beth Israel Temple and its rabbi, German-born Jacob Wechsler. Rabbi Wechsler served the congregation for several years in the late 1880s and early 1890s, and he was troubled by the increasing dichotomy between the town's wealthiest citizens and its poorest. When a $30,000 bond issue was proposed to build new schools for the white children of Meridian, Wechsler went to the mayor and city councilmen and pleaded for inclusion of a black school in the plan. His stand was unpopu-

In an era when race relations were deteriorating, Rabbi Jacob Wechsler fought for a bond issue which paid for the first publicly funded brick school for blacks in Mississippi.

lar; blacks were rapidly being disenfranchised and their education was considered unnecessary by many. Wechsler was persistent, and when the bond issue passed, a large part of it was designated for a new brick school in the black community. Grateful for his intervention, the parents proposed that it be named Wechsler School. The two-story brick structure, serving grades 1-8, opened in 1894. It was the first brick school for blacks funded by public bonds in Mississippi.

Just up the street from Wechsler, Professor G. M. Reese and his wife, Johnnie Pearl, were struggling to provide an even more ambitious educational opportunity for blacks. They started the Meridian Baptist Seminary in the basement of New Hope Baptist Church in 1896, later replacing it with a frame building on a high hill overlooking Wechsler School. As the school grew, Reese had his students bring old bricks each day, eventually accumulating enough to replace the wooden school with a two-story brick building. College-level courses and religious training were offered under the Reeses' leadership for almost fifty years.

Meridian exploded into the twentieth-century with the force of one of the dozens of locomotives which were steaming into town every day. Lumber from the region's great pine forests was fueling the economic cycle, along with the coal and iron coming from Alabama's mountains. Ten thousand railcars annually carried over 100,000,000 board feet of lumber from Meridian's mills. Factories sprang up to handle the by-products and textile mills absorbed much of the region's cotton production. In the midst of all this freight activity, forty passenger trains a day were pulling into the new Union Station in

Across the street from Wechsler, President Reese led Meridian Baptist Seminary through its most productive years in the 1920s and 1930s, but the school gradually diminished in scope and effectiveness following his death. Its last students left in 1972, and the bricks so diligently collected and mortared together by its students have been slowly crumbling since. A monument to Professor and Mrs. Reese stands in the side yard, framed by cedars bent into an archway by long-ago alumni.

The Jackson house fell on hard times along with Meridian; a series of owners after 1914 chopped its high-ceilinged rooms and wide hallways into apartments, and it was ready for demolition when it was taken over by the Meridian Restoration Foundation in 1968. Renamed "Merrehope" (Meridian/Restoration/Hope), it was stabilized and repainted and serves now as a fascinating mirror of Meridian's history.

Union Station's tower was the first impression of Meridian for decades of visitors arriving by train. As the trains disappeared, so did the utility of the station; the tower was pulled down in the 1940s and most of the station was demolished over the next twenty years. A resurgence in passenger travel along Amtrak lines brought renewed interest in Meridian's history as a rail center, and the station and tower were rebuilt in recent years. Its huge clock face and exposed brackets faithfully echo the original.

The Dentzel Carousel still delights children and adults; after years of neglect, the carved animals were sent off for restoration, one by one. The century-old gears continue to turn the planking, accompanied by a modern sound system which replaced the worn-out organ. Only two other similar stationary carousels survive in America, neither in their original buildings.

As Meridian grew away from downtown, retail patterns changed. Shopping centers and malls took much of the business away from the venerable Marks-Rothenberg store, and its doors closed in 1991. Acres of floors are empty, awaiting adaptive reuse. The façade, long hidden under modern aluminum, has been repaired and looks as new as the day the store opened in 1890.

A third-floor office door in Marks-Rothenberg was, for sixty years, the only access into the Grand Opera House. When a mannequin would crack or unsold merchandise was damaged, employees just opened the door and tossed the unwanted item into the cavernous darkness of the auditorium. The old storefront entrance of the Opera House was occupied by a shoe store, its back wall concealing the treasures within. Many older Meridianites remembered the Grand, but no one expected the sight which met them when that wall was finally taken down. As the plaster dust settled, flashlight beams lit up a theatrical time capsule. Dust covered every crevice and cobwebs hung in sheets from the balconies and the massive chandelier, but the integrity of the building was unchanged. The deep stage with its orchestra pit looked ready for a new production, and the catwalks still held the ropes to pull up the backdrops and lower the props. Even the trap door in the stage floor was intact. The lobby mirrors, which once reflected cutaway coats and high-button shoes, were still imbedded in the columns. As volunteers worked to clean up the interior, they found ancient gum wrappers and candy boxes, even a program from Sarah Bernhardt's 1892 performance of *La Tosca*.

The Grand Opera House, once the symbol of Meridian's success, was ready for an encore. All over town, historic preservation efforts have brought the resurgent city back to life by emphasizing the past. The shiny new tower of Union Station, the repainted lions of the Dentzel Carousel, even Juriah Jackson's hidden pioneer house deep within Merrehope, reflect the past that explains the present. And someday the Grand Opera House will again welcome famous actors and enthusiastic audiences, shining once more as the Pride of Meridian.

Pass Christian

Win'Rush

Pass Christian took its name from one of two deep-water passes which flowed between the mainland and the barrier islands.

On sultry summer days a century ago, thousands of vacationers strolled the beaches and oak-lined streets of Pass Christian, enjoying the sun and sea breezes. This was the most popular resort on the Gulf of Mexico, pulling in tourists from all over the South and points north.

Most guests stayed in one of the luxurious, sprawling hotels facing the Gulf. Two hundred and fifty rooms at the Mexican Gulf were usually full; those looking for more intimate inns could choose the Magnolia or the Lynne Castle. Scenic Drive was lined with the mansions and cottages of semi-permanent residents, rich New Orleanians and Louisiana planters who retreated to the Mississippi coast for relaxation every weekend.

One hundred years later, the great hotels of Pass Christian are long gone, victims of fire and hurricanes and the exodus of the tourist trade to Florida. All that remains of the town's heyday as America's Southern Riviera are the Scenic Drive homes, an astonishingly varied collection of twenty-seven architectural styles stretching along a three-mile vista.

When d'Iberville's expedition sailed by here in 1699, the narrow peninsula between the Gulf and Bay St. Louis was home only to Indians and a variety of wildlife. A few of the French explorers chose to stay here, and three hundred years later their influence is evident in the street names and telephone listings with a French flair. In the 1740s, Christian and Marianne Ladnier settled on Cat Island, and their names were given to the two deep water passes which run parallel to the main shoreline. The village which grew up on the mainland was also called Pass Christian.

Home to only Indians and wildlife nearly 300 years ago, the narrow peninsula dubbed Pass Christian became America's Southern Riviera and is still active today as a resort and vacationer's paradise.

A landmark since the 1850s, the original Trinity Episcopal Church was blown away during Hurricane Camille. Parishoners built this identical reproduction soon afterwards.

The Mississippi coast passed repeatedly from the hands of one European power to another throughout the 1700s, finally becoming a Spanish possession in 1781. The Spanish crown granted most of the Pass Christian area to Frenchman François Carrierre. His wife, whose knack for outliving three husbands earned her the nickname "the Widow Asmard," inherited the land from François. When she died in the late 1790s, the huge tract of property was divided between her nephew, Benjamin Pellerin, and two of her freed slaves, Charlot and Madelon Asmard. Every lot in Pass Christian can be traced back to one of these two bequests.

In 1810, Spain acquiesced to pressure from West Floridians and deeded the Mississippi coast to the United States. Dr. William Flood raised the American flag over Pass Christian the following year. Within three short years, that American affiliation placed the little town in peril; British warships with 10,000 men anchored offshore as Andrew Jackson's army marched toward New Orleans. When he won his famous battle there, the War of 1812 had already ended, but his fame was assured.

General Jackson was welcomed into New Orleans in a victory celebration coordinated by Edward Livingston, a prominent New Orleans lawyer. Livingston was one of the first Crescent City residents to recognize the vacation potential of the Gulf Coast, and he arranged to purchase the bulk of Benjamin Pellerin's estate. His was the first of the elaborate summer homes to appear on what would later be called Scenic Drive. Livingston had a limited amount of time to spend in either New Orleans or Pass Christian; he served as President Jackson's Secretary of State and died in Paris while serving as the American Ambassador to France.

After Livingston's death in 1836, his widow sold the Pass Christian land to John Henderson and two other men. Like Livingston, Henderson would build a mansion on Scenic Drive, but he went one step further than his predecessor. He divided the entire peninsula into lots and began marketing them widely. In 1838, Pass Christian had grown enough to be formally incorporated as a town. It already had the first of its massive hotels. The Pass Christian Hotel had opened in 1831 and gradually grew to include a dining room, ballroom, billiard room, bowling alley, and stables. Wings were added onto the original hotel block, leading to a tremendous U-shaped complex with hundreds of chambers. In 1849, the first regatta in the South sailed from the hotel's pier; sailors came from Bay St. Louis, Biloxi, Mississippi City, Mobile, New Orleans, Pensacola and Pascagoula. Enthusiasm was high and the Southern Yacht Club was formed as the first in the South. It soon moved to New Orleans, leaving the Pass Christian Yacht Club as a loosely organized entity.

By 1850, Pass Christian was a prosperous town with two thousand year-round residents. Steamboats traveling from Mobile to New Orleans made regular stops, and crops and manufactured goods from inland Mississippi were carted to the piers of Pass Christian for shipment. The Scenic Drive road was sporting

Live Oak Cemetery is an ancient burial ground which holds the remains of Revolutionary War veterans, Pass Christian's earliest settlers and a governor of Louisiana.

Greek Revival mansions and Italianate cottages, all facing the Gulf waters through a screen of live oaks. John Henderson had prospered enough to be philanthropic; he donated land for Trinity Episcopal Church and its neighboring graveyard, Live Oak Cemetery. Live Oak was actually an older burying ground, already holding the remains of Revolutionary War veterans and early settlers, but Henderson's support allowed it to be improved. Obelisk-

War Memorial Park is filled with live oaks, each named for a figure in American history. Its gazebo is shaded by "George Washington," "Abraham Lincoln," and "Betsy Ross."

The live oaks in War Memorial Park are named for historical figures.

like pillars framed a carriage gate with a cross-topped arch. The grounds were filled with the massive trees which inspired its name, interspersed with granite and cypresswood markers and above-ground tombs. Wrought-iron cornstalk fences enclosed family plots. The northernmost area was "set aside as free ground for the interment of both white and black." Trinity Episcopal Church was finished in 1850, a tiny Gothic chapel with only sanctuary space. Within years, a rear gallery and transepts were added.

Like towns throughout the state, Pass Christian saw a burst of homebuilding on a grand scale immediately before the Civil War brought a halt to Mississippi's prosperity. One of the last antebellum homes to be built on Scenic Drive was Pierre Saucier's two-story Greek Revival house. Saucier was the son of one of Pass Christian's first settlers and he had purchased a lot on Scenic Drive in 1839. When he finally built his mansion, it was an impressive structure with a pedimented portico set in front of an inset gallery. Cast iron-filigrees formed the balustrades lining the porch.

Saucier was barely settled into his new house, along with his son, daughter-in-law and several children, when Mississippi seceded from the Union. Word reached the coast of the wild celebrations greeting the news in Jackson, and the adoption of the "Bonnie Blue Flag" as the first official Confederate banner. A group of Pass Christian ladies sewed up a copy of the flag and raised it on the pole fronting the Saucier home. Union troops who landed on the beaches in 1862 did not find this display appropriate. They commandeered the Sauciers' house as their headquarters and exiled the family to the upstairs rooms. Confederates to fight were scarce, and boredom soon set in. The Union officers asked if anyone in the house could play the grand piano in the parlor; Saucier's daughter-in-law obliged. Sitting at the keys, she defiantly banged out "The Bonnie Blue Flag," then flounced upstairs to take care of her newborn son (who would, incidentally, grow up to become mayor of Pass Christian). When the Union troops left, they took the flag with them.

War left few scars on the coast, and Pass Christian quickly recovered. Building resumed along Scenic Drive. Until 1869, visitors usually came by carriage, effectively limiting the trade to Louisiana, Mississippi and Alabama residents. In 1869, that changed dramatically. The New Orleans, Mobile and Chattanooga Railroad laid its lines through Pass Christian, connecting it with the entire Southeast and North. In most towns, railroads were important as a means to ship goods and products out. In Pass Christian, they were a means to bring people in. That is exactly what happened; as northerners eager to escape the colder climates began to travel to the coast, word spread of this resort town. Within a few years, Pass Christian was building not only millionaires' homes but enormous hotels. The largest was the Mexican Gulf with 250 rooms. Its main entrance was

During Federal occupation of Pass Christian, Mrs. Saucier defiantly played Confederate battle songs for Union soldiers occupying her home.

This was where the greatest pleasure in the world was to watch the pelicans dive for fish from the shade of a wide front porch.

The three-mile stretch of Scenic Drive paralleling the beach is one of Mississippi's most beautiful historic districts. Twenty-seven different architectural styles are represented, all surrounded by live oaks and colorful gardens.

fronted by a monumental semicircular portico and archways leading to verandahs.

Vacationers poured in by the trainload. By 1900, the summer population of Pass Christian was over 8000, with sailing, gambling, horse racing, cock fighting and hunting on the entertainment agenda. New Orleanians considered this their personal corner of the coast, and each day found a 3:00 p.m. "Banker's Special" running from downtown New Orleans to Pass Christian.

Architects were kept busy designing the houses along Scenic Drive. Neoclassic and Queen Anne styles joined the old Greek Revival and Italianate homes. Porches and picket fences became a tradition. Lawns were showplaces, with carefully tended azaleas and camellias.

Pass Christian was riding high, but its day in the sun was limited. The Gulf and Ship Island Railroad was finally completed from Jackson to Gulfport in 1902; when Gulfport deepened its harbor, the commercial trade left Pass Christian. An even more serious blow was the development of

The wide front porches of Scenic Drive's historic homes are the perfect spot for watching pelicans and sailboats in the Gulf.

Florida's Gulf Coast, with its wider, whiter beaches. As the tourist trade dwindled, the great hotels fell into disrepair. A series of fires and hurricanes destroyed them all between 1915 and 1919. Occasional attempts were later made to revive the tradition. The Grey Castle opened in a huge Victorian home in 1922 and Inn-by-the-Sea was built on Henderson Point in 1927, but neither achieved the success of the originals.

As the tourist dollars flowed elsewhere, businesses and community strength in Pass Christian suffered. Churches had depended as much as any other institution on the thousands of visitors each year, and Trinity Episcopal struggled through the early years of the twentieth century. Live Oak Cemetery was filled with veterans of every American war and even the grave of George Washington's niece, but its church was barely surviving. Rector Nowell Logan took over the parish in 1900 and waged a valiant fight to keep the congregation going for the next twenty-four years. The old Gothic chapel was sadly in need of attention, and his journals reflect his concerns: "Things I want done in the Parish: 1) A large square tower without spire in front...of the Church . . . say, fifteen feet square to look then like old English Church and to take the place of the little belfry which is dangerous. The whole Church, back to the Vestry room shakes when the bell is rung." A later notation reflects his disappointment with the results of his tower campaign: "Did not get it but Porch instead." The congregation was dwindling along with the physical plant: "No one came to Early Service . . . only one person came to Holy Communion . . . No one came to the Library Service . . . the offering $8.50."

When Reverend Logan died in 1924, the plot where he was buried in Live Oak Cemetery wasn't much quieter than the rest of Pass Christian. The town was still a favorite spot for the rich and famous, having hosted President Woodrow Wilson in 1913 and former President Theodore Roosevelt in 1915. "Advice to the Lovelorn" columnist Dorothy Dix kept a permanent home on

Scenic Drive, and the Banker's Special ran until World War II took its cars away as troop trains.

That war led to the dedication of War Memorial Park in 1944. Each of its live oaks was registered and given a name, such as "George Washington," "Betsy Ross" and "Jefferson Davis." In the harbor, the long-dormant Pass Christian Yacht Club had been revived, and it sponsored frequent regattas and water activities. In 1950, Highway 90 was four-laned and new sand pumped in to expand the beaches lining it. Pass Christian was a quieter, more refined counterpart to the larger coast towns like Biloxi and Gulfport.

Pass Christian would have remained a small town, welcoming the same summer guests who showed up every spring to air out the old Scenic Drive houses and build their bonfires on the beach. Shops downtown catered to an upscale clientele and nothing much varied from year to year.

All that changed in one terrifying night in August, 1969. Hurricane Camille had been churning through the Caribbean and Gulf of Mexico for days, building up strength until it reached record-breaking intensity. As it took aim at the Mississippi Coast, residents fled northward, unsure whether it would head east toward Alabama or west toward New Orleans. It did neither. With two-hundred-mile-an-hour winds and towering waves, it smashed directly into Pass Christian, devastating the coast for miles in either direction and all but obliterating whole sections of the old resort town. Hundred-year-old mansions on Scenic Drive were crushed into rubble; live oaks which had shaded French explorers were ripped up by the roots and toppled into the flooded streets. Trinity Episcopal's sanctuary exploded, killing the caretaker, thirteen members of his family and the pastor's wife. Plots in Live Oak were washed away.

The South's first yacht club was established in Pass Christian in 1849. It has endured for a century-and-a-half and boasts one of the Coast's finest small craft harbors.

The next morning, sixty-six people in Pass Christian were dead. The town itself was almost unrecognizable; entire blocks of buildings were gone, their remnants blown miles into Mississippi. Only the steps of Trinity remained, and the Saucier House had been heavily damaged. War Memorial Park looked more like a war zone. There was no evidence that the Yacht Club had ever existed at all.

As Mississippi and the nation mobilized to send aid, no one would have blamed Pass Christianers for turning their backs on the unpredictable Gulf which could spawn such destruction. There were other places to live where Nature would not wipe out all of a life's treasures in a split second. But this was Pass Christian; this was where the greatest pleasure in the world was to watch the pelicans dive for fish from the shade of a wide front porch, and the spectacular sunsets outweighed the danger of an occasional hurricane. Before the first post-Camille day was over, tiny American flags were sprouting in what had been fine lawns, each signaling the owner's intentions to rebuild. Debris was hauled away, unsalvageable homes were demolished, and Pass Christian moved on.

The scars of Hurricane Camille are now all but gone. Trinity Episcopal Church has been rebuilt, an identical replica of the 1850 building which Reverend Logan loved so much. The oaks in the cemetery replanted after the storm have soared, as have those in War Memorial Park. It's still evident which trees are four hundred years old and which ones are only thirty, but it doesn't much matter. Anything planted in this gracious corner of Mississippi has a way of falling in step with the overall atmosphere of serenity and natural beauty. Scenic Drive remains the most breathtaking three miles on the coast, a lasting gift from those long-gone visitors who recognized paradise when they saw it.

Ocean Springs

Walter Anderson
Mural

As young artists in the 1930s, brothers Mac and Walter Anderson were commissioned to decorate the Jacobean Revival Ocean Springs High School. Since the school's closing, the murals have been relocated to the Walter Anderson Museum of Art.

Ocean Springs keeps getting rediscovered. First the French, then rich New Orleanians, later winter-weary Chicagoans and finally art lovers have arrived in sequential waves, overwhelmed by the beauty of this seaside community. Each group has left its mark, molding Ocean Springs into one of the most unique and visually unforgettable towns in Mississippi.

As far as European settlement in Mississippi goes, it all started right here, on the east side of Biloxi Bay. Pierre Lemoyne Sieur d'Iberville wasn't particularly interested in the beaches and sunshine of the Gulf Coast when he sailed his little fleet of four ships into the Mississippi Sound in 1699. He was looking for the mouth of the Mississippi River, which La Salle had brazenly claimed for France in 1682 without having a clue to its location. D'Iberville's men anchored on Ship Island and spent several months searching for the river delta. When it came time for d'Iberville to report back to France, he chose a site on the east side of Biloxi Bay to build a fort. There certainly wasn't much to protect, and no visible enemies from which to protect it. The Indians were friendly enough, and the Spanish and English were at a safe distance, but this was a strange new world and d'Iberville wasn't taking any chances. He put his men to work cutting trees and hauling them onto the beach. A rectangular palisade with corner bastions was fortified with cannons unloaded from the French frigates. When Fort Maurepas was finished, d'Iberville sailed east, leaving Sauvole de la Villantry in charge of seventy-six men and ten officers. His second-in-command was d'Iberville's younger brother, Bienville. Mississippi's first European settlement, though modest, was a reality.

Palisaded Fort Maurepas, Mississippi's first European settlement, was lost after the French moved their capital to Biloxi and then New Orleans. A replica of the fort was built in the 1980s.

When D'Iberville returned in 1700, he found Sauvole dead of yellow fever and Bienville in charge of the fort. It had been a hard summer and fall for the French soldiers. The breezes blowing in off the Mississippi Sound helped to relieve the stifling heat, but they also brought hordes of insects and disease-bearing mosquitoes. The water flowing out of Fort Bayou was brackish at best, and the men d'Iberville found hanging on at Fort Maurepas were desperate to relocate. In 1702, the settlement was moved to Mobile Bay, leaving only a handful of intrepid settlers behind.

With French support gone, the east side of Biloxi Bay was quiet. The French government would briefly return here in 1719, but soon after moved on to "New Biloxey" and then New Orleans. For over one hundred years, the site of Fort Maurepas would be forgotten. The palisades may have been washed into the bay or intentionally destroyed. A few fishermen and charcoal burners made their homes here, but access to the growing community of Biloxi was difficult and most people settled on the west side of the bay.

In the first decades of the nineteenth century, the future site of Ocean Springs was "rediscovered" for the first time. Steamboats had first appeared at New Orleans' wharves in 1812, the same year that the Gulf Coast was annexed to the Mississippi Territory. These ships revolutionized traffic up and down the Mississippi River and along the Gulf of Mexico. They required frequent stops for refueling and to take on fresh water, and the peninsula jutting into Biloxi Bay was a logical stopping point on the Mobile-to-New Orleans run. Refueling was a slow process, so travelers would stretch their legs along the dirt roads leading from the beach into the unnamed village.

In 1835, Harriet Porter came up with the bright idea of building a

Schuyler Poitevent spent a lifetime collecting relics along the beaches of Biloxi Bay. He was convinced that old Fort Maurepas had existed on his land.

The traffic from New Orleans had revitalized Ocean Springs, and the Crescent City's wealth and social tradition would strongly influence the development and atmosphere of the town for more than a century.

beachfront hotel to hold some of those travelers a bit longer. Her Ocean Springs Hotel faced oak-lined Jackson Avenue and backed up to the beach. It quickly attracted the attention of New Orleanians who wanted a weekend getaway. Some of those who enjoyed their stay on Biloxi Bay decided to build weekend homes, and the growing community quickly took on a New Orleans flavor. Tourism increased when mineral springs were discovered along Fort Bayou, their waters touted as being "especially efficacious in cases of dyspepsia, indigestion, insomnia and the many kindred ailments." In 1852 a post office was established as "Lynchburg Springs." Within a year, the townspeople had changed that to the more alluring "Ocean Springs," with the town taking its name from Mrs. Porter's very successful hostelry.

The traffic from New Orleans had revitalized Ocean Springs, and the Crescent City's wealth and social traditions would strongly influence the development and atmosphere of the town for more than a century. The Civil War came and went without any structural damage to the

The original L&N train depot was probably destroyed by a hurricane in the early years of the twentieth century. This structure was completed in 1907 and now houses the Chamber of Commerce.

New Orleans matron Louisa Bartlett spent every summer in Ocean Springs and led the drive to establish a permanent church, Ocean Springs Presbyterian, in the resort community.

community, although steamboat traffic was disrupted and the subsequent loss of tourist trade temporarily halted growth. No one really paid much attention to the Union boats anchored at Ship Island. When the war ended, the steamboat trade picked up again and Ocean Springs was back in business.

As vital as the seagoing tourist trade had been, it paled in comparison to what was coming for the entire Gulf Coast. In 1867, surveyors fanned out from New Orleans and Mobile, plotting the proposed routes for the New Orleans, Mobile and Chattanooga Railroad. By 1870, the trains were running back and forth along the coast, and Ocean Springs was set for its most prosperous period. It was just far enough from New Orleans to be a true vacation getaway, yet close enough that those New Orleanians with money to burn could reasonably build accessible estate homes on the water. One of the first to do so was a native Mississippian, Junius Poitevent, who had married into New Orleans wealth. His family ran a Hancock County sawmill at Gainesville; in 1877 Poitevent used lumber from that mill to build the Greek Revival "Bay Home" in the section of Ocean Springs which would come to be known as Lover's Lane. Poitevent was successful in a variety of business ventures and his taste is reflected in the details of the home, designed with concave soffits to deflect hurricane winds. Poitevent's son, Schuyler, developed a lifelong fascination with artifacts while wandering the beaches fronting Bay Home. He collected thousands of objects for his collection and held firm to the likely theory that the original Fort Maurepas was on his family land.

The New Orleans, Mobile and Chattanooga Railroad was taken over by the L&N in the 1880s, and a depot was built to serve the passenger trains which arrived daily. New commercial and residential streets grew up around the depot, with Washington Avenue developing into the primary downtown thoroughfare. More boarding houses were going up to rival the Ocean Springs Hotel, including the Artesia and the Frye House. With more people moving in every day and the hotels jammed to capacity, ancillary services were needed. Jacques Bertuccini was a Croatian immigrant who moved from New Orleans in 1896 to tap into the booming climate in Ocean Springs as a barber. He built a quaint Queen Anne cottage on Washington Street next door to his barbershop. The Bertuccini House was placed on brick piers and fronted with a cross gable roof. Turned posts with sawn brackets support a deep U-shaped porch. Mr. Bertuccini must have been successful; within a few years of opening his business, he was advertising the installation of new fixtures and two new barber chairs.

New Orleans wasn't the only big city with its eye on Ocean Springs. As railroads connected the Old South with the Midwest, Chicagoans eager for sun were more and more willing to make the twenty-four hour trip to the coast. Several wealthy Chicago families bought up land along Biloxi Bay for summer estates, including Louis Sullivan, America's premier late-nineteenth century architect. He may have had some influence on the style of St. John's Episcopal Church, constructed in 1892 from plans in *Churchman Magazine*. The design combined High Victorian Gothic details with Queen Anne and Shingle elements, accented with articulated buttresses and Gothic-arched windows of etched glass.

Nearby was the First Presbyterian Church, completed with the financial and spiritual backing of Louisa Burling Bartlett. Mrs. Bartlett was a well-to-do New Orleans matron who had been spending her summers in Ocean

St. John's Episcopal Church, Mississippi's finest example of High Victorian Gothic architecture, was completed in 1892.

Ocean Springs' fortunes took off when it became one of the most popular day-trip destinations of the newly completed New Orleans-to-Mobile railroad. The railroad donated the land for the establishment of Marshall Park in 1911.

Spring, since 1853. Along with the rest of Ocean Springs' Presbyterians, she had been "borrowing" the Baptist Church for services since Civil War days. Determined to have a true Presbyterian Church in her summer hometown before she died, she invited seven other families into her home in 1886 to plan for a new sanctuary. The one-story wood frame Greek Revival chapel was completed in 1886, and Mrs. Bartlett had a chance to enjoy it for three years before her death.

The twentieth century found Ocean Springs at its peak, with excursion trains running from New Orleans twice a week. Hackney cabs lined up at the depot to transport the daytrippers to the beach and overnight guests to hotels. Richer clients from New Orleans and Chicago appeared each June to spend the season in their summer houses. In 1906, a devastating hurricane destroyed several hotels and many private homes, and probably did irreparable damage to the L&N Depot. A new depot was built in 1907, and in 1911, the city leased the land lining the tracks for the establishment of Marshall Park. Its bandstand was busy throughout the summer with concerts and performances.

The good times lasted only a few more years. Several of the hotels, including the original Ocean Springs, were lost to fire. Florida was engaged in an all-out effort to build up its beaches and attract the southern tourist trade. Highways were pulling business away from the railroads, and bit by bit the depot fell into disuse, along with Marshall Park. The Great Depression hit New Orleans hard, and the steady flow of money from that city to Ocean Springs began to dry up. Ocean Springs was slowly being forgotten once again.

One positive effect of the Depression was a WPA program for artists. Peter Anderson had founded Shearwater Pottery on his family's estate in the late 1920s; his brothers, Walter and Mac, were already turning out ceramics

Through the years, artist Walter Anderson would achieve great fame producing striking paintings of the coast's wildlife and history.

The history and wildlife of the Gulf Coast are depicted on the walls of the Ocean Springs Community Center in striking murals painted by artist Walter Anderson in 1951.

and textiles of extraordinary originality when the nation's economic crisis disrupted their business. The WPA provided the brothers with work in decorating the new Ocean Springs High School, completed in 1927. Mac spent two years creating a tile mural, "Fish and Birds," in the foyer. Walter was busy in the auditorium, painting oil-on-canvas panels for the mural, "Ocean Springs, Past and Present." Through the years, Walter Anderson would achieve the greatest fame, producing striking paintings of the coast's wildlife and history. In 1951, he spent months drawing and painting vivid, intertwining murals depicting the history and wildlife of the area on the walls of the Ocean Springs Community Center.

Ocean Springs High School closed in May, 1965, and the Anderson murals began to deteriorate as the elements intruded on the old building. A few blocks away, the depot had lost its purpose when the last passenger train left for New Orleans. The building was converted into the Chamber of Commerce, which was faced with the challenge of promoting a town which was no longer a tourist mecca and had lost its New Orleans trade to more fashionable spots. The challenge was answered through the gradual development of Ocean Springs into an artists' mecca. The murals were removed from the high school and placed in the new Walter Anderson Museum of Art. The old shops and homes along Washington Avenue filled with paintings, pottery and antiques.

The French explorers have been gone for three hundred years. Their fort is a memory, replaced by a replica on Front Beach. Perhaps the remains of the original are in Schuyler Poitevent's front yard, and that would be a truly historic treasure to uncover. But the real treasure in Ocean Springs is the beauty of the town itself, a jewel repeatedly discovered and improved by three centuries of Mississippians.

Hattiesburg

Hattiesburg Depot

The Art Deco Forrest Hotel was completed in the late 1920s and featured running ice water and fans in every room.

There's a faded aerial view of Tatum Lumber Company, taken sometime during the four decades when it ran nonstop in the woods south of Hattiesburg. The noise and clamor of logging radiate from the photo; a huge multi-story mill is spewing smoke and logs barrel down flues into the water. Locomotives trundle along short dummy lines, special railroads built just to haul the hundred-foot pines from the deep forests into the mill. In its heyday, Tatum Lumber ran twenty-four hours a day, carving the Piney Woods into homes for a surging country.

The mill is long gone, a victim of dwindling forests and dwindling demand. All that remains are a few scattered buildings, quiet survivors of the hundreds which once lined the dirt roads of this company town. The commissary shelves are empty and only the metal bread sign on the screen door gives a clue to the business which once went on here. A hundred feet away, the old office building looks like a camp lodge. The tiny window where the manager would dole out "brozeen," the mill worker's hard-earned currency, has been closed for decades. Almost hidden in the underbrush, the doctor's office is tilting precariously on its foundation.

In October, 1893, what little there was of Hattiesburg burned to the ground. Within two weeks, the city fathers passed an ordinance forbidding construction of any but fireproof buildings. Hattiesburg wasn't the first or the last town to pass such an edict. In those days of questionable water supplies and horsedrawn fire wagons, it just made sense. What was odd was that even as the aldermen were signing their names to the decree, Tatum Lumber

Oaks District, Hattiesburg's first "suburb," was built on cutover pine lands between 1900 and 1915. The homeowners pulled up pine stumps and planted water oaks which have grown into towering shade trees.

Architect Robert E. Lee designed many of Hattiesburg's most notable public buildings, including the 1911 and 1921 segments of the old Hattiesburg High School.

Company was just getting started, joining J. J. Newman Lumber Company in an all-out assault on the surrounding forests. The pine boards they produced would propel Hattiesburg from a burned-out village to Mississippi's fourth-largest city in just a decade.

The "cow counties" of southeast Mississippi, four million acres in all, had been one of the first Choctaw cessions, dating back to 1805. Endless pine forests, with 100-foot-tall trees packed so closely together that light never hit the ground, covered much of the area. What open land there was wouldn't support much of a cotton crop, so this was not prime territory for settlement in the years before the Civil War. The land along the Leaf and Bouie rivers, halfway between Jackson and the Gulf Coast, was quiet until the clang of steel rails approached in the 1880s.

W. H. Hardy was a railroad pioneer, a Meridian lawyer who had helped build that tiny town into the state's railroad center. His position as vice-president and chief engineer of the proposed New Orleans and Northeast Railroad took him deep into the forests of south Mississippi, scouting out the best route to lay the tracks. Walking along the banks of the Leaf River one day in 1883, Hardy began to visualize a waystation where the NO&NE would eventually cross a Gulf Coast-to-Jackson line. He bought up the land around Gordon's Crossing, sketched the site onto his grids, and directed his crews up the line from New Orleans. Within a year, two hundred and fifty settlers had joined him and a town was incorporated as "Hattiesburg" in honor of Hardy's wife.

The new town struggled for a decade. One rail line wasn't enough to ignite the lumber industry, and the area had little else to offer except solitude. But America was entering a period of rapid growth, consuming building materials as fast as they could be supplied, and yellow pine lumber was in increasing demand. Pennsylvania lumberman Fenwick Peck came to Hattiesburg in 1893 to check out the facilities of the J. J. Newman Lumber

Company, recently built on the site of the burned-out Wiscasset Mill. Peck saw unlimited potential in the mill and unlimited resources in the Piney Woods belt stretching across south Mississippi. He began clearing title to the surrounding pine lands. Hot on his heels was W. S. F. Tatum, a Tennessee native who joined with his brother-in-law to build Tatum-O'Neal Lumber Mill. Between them, these two enterprises would dominate the industry which would eventually consume Mississippi's Pine Belt. Newman controlled over 400,000 acres of timber, felling it and feeding it into its huge operation along the Leaf River on the northeast edge of town. Twelve hundred mill workers turned the towering logs into lumber, shipping it out on long rail cars. An entire community grew up within the mill, including housing, stores, machine shops and an independent water and fire protection system. The mills ran endlessly, producing 75 million board feet of lumber annually.

Hattiesburg was poised to grow, and the 1897 completion of the Gulf and Ship Island Railroad from Gulfport to Jackson provided the final spark. Thousands of loggers swarmed through the dense forests, stacking the giant trees onto "dummy lines" to run back into Hattiesburg. Dressed out as finished lumber, the pine then headed for the coast, where Gulfport had grown into the nation's largest port for yellow pine.

Fueled by the insatiable demand for its product, Hattiesburg was expanding into the cutover areas surrounding downtown. North Main Street was lined with mansions of the lumber barons, Queen Anne turrets and towers competing with the columns of Neoclassicism. John McLeod was a young merchant who had moved from Purvis in 1896. With his business booming from the lumber-driven economy, he built the exuberant house at

W. S. F. Tatum came to Hattiesburg in the 1890s and built a lumbering empire, Tatum Lumber Company, which ran 24 hours a day.

Businessman John McLeod's Queen Anne house is a riot of towers, balconies and porches. It is the last of the exuberant mansions which once lined North Main Street.

220 • HATTIESBURG

North Main Street was lined with mansions of the lumber barons, Queen Anne turrets competing with the columns of Neoclassicism.

803 North Main. Its two-and-a-half stories were a riot of towers, balconies and porches, all outlined with gingerbread trim. Across the street, W. S. F. Tatum built an enormous Neoclassical mansion surrounded by curving porches.

In the Oaks District, homeowners dug up pine stumps and planted water oaks along the brick streets. Hattiesburg was home to two companies which mass-produced the elements of Craftsman bungalows, one of the most popular styles for middle-class families in the early 1900s. The Aladdin Company and the Gordon Van Tine Company provided the materials for many of the new homes in the Oaks District. Streetcars radiated out from downtown to carry the "commuters" of these early suburbs to work.

In the brief period between 1900 and 1908, Hattiesburg's population tripled. Forrest County was carved out of Perry County and Hattiesburg was the logical choice as the new county seat. Local architect Robert E. Lee was working overtime to build the public buildings which such status required, as well as private homes. He designed the new City Hall and the Masonic

Mississippi Normal College was awarded to Hattiesburg after the city offered $250,000 and several hundred acres of cutover pine land to the state. R. H. Hunt designed five classical buildings for the 1912 campus, including the first president's home.

Temple, along with numerous office buildings to house the thirty lumber wholesale companies filling downtown. A new Hattiesburg High School was built on North Main in 1911, replacing an older structure which had been quickly outgrown.

South Mississippi was catching up with the older parts of Mississippi in population and power. Both of the state's universities were in north Mississippi, and in 1910 the legislature sanctioned the creation of a third public college. In a typically cryptic move, no money was appropriated for the institution. Counties and towns were invited to make their best offer. Hattiesburg and Forrest County came forward with $250,000 and several hundred acres of cutover pine land donated by local businessmen. The offer was accepted, and R. H. Hunt was hired to design a new campus on the west edge of town. His plan placed five classically inspired buildings on a sweeping drive beginning at the last Hardy Street streetcar stop. The buildings were ready for classes in the fall of 1912, and Mississippi Normal College opened with a faculty of eighteen and two hundred and twenty students. Full degrees would not be offered until 1922.

The addition of a college was a feather in Hattiesburg's cap, but it could not long defer the economic consequences looming over the Pine Belt. The forests were thinning at an alarming rate, decimated by twenty years of wholesale logging. The area was granted a temporary reprieve with the opening of Camp Shelby. When America entered World War I in 1917, training bases were an immediate need. Dr. W. W. Crawford led the drive to bring one of those facilities to Hattiesburg.

The Saenger Theatre is the only one of several downtown movie palaces to have survived urban change. It now houses a community theatre and art museum.

Newman Lumber Company provided the land, Dr. Crawford's connections sealed the deal, and overnight an entire military town rose in the woods south of Hattiesburg. Forty thousand troops provided a healthy boost to the local economy.

Camp Shelby would be shuttered by 1919; more devastating to Hattiesburg was the depletion of the pine forests. Thousands of acres of trees had been cleared; when the mills slowed down, Hattiesburg's unemployment lines grew. Residential construction slowed drastically. One of the few significant public buildings to emerge in the 1920s was an enlarged Hattiesburg High School. Robert E. Lee, known for his classical models, hooked a massive Jacobean Revival brick school to the front of the 1911 structure, dominated by a four-story tower and braced by corner entrances designating "Boys" and "Girls."

By the time Depression gripped the rest of Mississippi, Hattiesburg had been struggling for a number of years. City leaders, desperate to bring passengers off the trains pulling up at the depot, supported the construction of downtown's Forrest Hotel, complete with running ice water and fans in every room. Monumental eagles capped the corners of its roof. Its Art Deco façade was complemented by the new Saenger Theatre next door. Glazed terra cotta tiles and cast-iron frieze work beckoned theatre goers into the 1100-seat auditorium to cool off and watch movies and plays, accompanied by the Mighty Morton Pipe Organ.

In the late 1930s, both Newman Lumber Company and Tatum Lumber Company finally closed, their supplies of pine almost totally depleted. Their housing was sold off and the great mills dismantled, leaving only ghostly remnants of the company towns which once thrived within their gates. The future of Hattiesburg looked bleak. At its lowest ebb, it was once again

Once a thriving community unto itself, the site of Tatum Lumber Company is now only an empty store, a crumbling doctor's office and the old main building, surrounded by towering pines.

revived by war. Pearl Harbor brought Camp Shelby back to life, with a call for 5000 workers going out. A thousand buildings and almost two hundred miles of roads were built, and fifty thousand soldiers poured in. On nights and weekends, Hattiesburg's streets were packed with jeeps and G.I.s. The Saenger and four other downtown movie houses were full every night.

Hattiesburg's economy, given a breather by Camp Shelby, gradually diversified enough to withstand the death of the lumber mills. The town grew west, leaving many of the old neighborhoods behind. The McLeod House was converted into office space; its neighbor, the Tatum House, is long gone. The Saenger lost its business to suburban theatres, and it closed its doors in 1974. The City of Hattiesburg now owns it, utilizing its stage for public events and its storefronts as an art gallery. Hattiesburg High School graduated its last class in 1960, serving for many years as an administration building before being sold to private interests. Mississippi Southern grew into the University of Southern Mississippi, its campus enveloping the five original R. H. Hunt buildings.

On the fringes of Hattiesburg, the remnants of the great lumber mills which built the town gradually disappeared. In 1971, the main office of the old Newman Lumber Company burned, destroying the last evidence of Mississippi's largest timber business. At the end of Newman Street and Buschman Street, a few company houses stand as reminders of the sprawling operation which once lined the riverbank.

Pines replanted fifty years ago now shade the empty offices of Tatum Lumber Company. They are in no danger of falling to the chainsaws of progress. The timber industry has moved on, leaving this quiet corner of the forest to slowly close in on the temporary evidence of man's attempt to control nature.

Bibliography

*M*uch of the background material for this book was obtained from the Historic Preservation files at the Mississippi Department of Archives and History. Many of these sites are on the National Register of Historic Places, and those lengthy nomination forms are included in the files, along with site descriptions, newspaper clippings, photographs, etc. Stories of each town were gathered through interviews with individuals in those towns. Other references are as follows:

GENERAL RESOURCES

Crocker, Mary Wallace. *Historic Architecture in Mississippi*. Jackson: University Press of Mississippi, 1973.

Gurney, Bill. *Mississippi's Courthouses, Then and Now*. Ripley: Old Timer Press, 1987.

Howell, Elmo. *Mississippi Home Places*. N.p., n.d.

——. *Mississippi Scenes*. N.p., n.d.

——. *Mississippi Backroads*. N.p., n.d.

Lane, Mills. *Architecture of the Old South: Mississippi/Alabama*. New York: Abbeville Press, 1989.

McLemore, Richard A., ed. *A History of Mississippi*. Jackson: University Press of Mississippi , 1973.

Rowland, Dunbar. *Mississippi*. 2 vols. 1907. Spartanburg: The Reprint Company, 1976.

Works Progress Administration. *Mississippi: The WPA Guide to the Magnolia State*. 1938. Reprint: University Press of Mississippi, 1988.

BROOKHAVEN

Brookhaven Centennial Historical Program, 1959.

Crawford, William F. Interview by Henry Ledet. Lincoln-Lawrence-Franklin Regional Library System, 1996.

Whitworth College Historical Sketch. Anonymous.

CARROLLTON

James, Timothy R., ed. *Carroll County: Looking Back Through the Years*. Winona, Ms: Montgomery Publishing, 1998.

Smith, Frank E. *The Yazoo River*. 1954. Reprint, Jackson: University Press of Mississippi, 1988.

Smith, J. Frazer. *White Pillars: The Architecture of the South*. New York: Bramhall House, 1941.

Williams Landing/Carroll County. Williams Landing Sesquicentennial, 1983.

COLUMBUS

Kaye, Samuel H., Rufus Ward, Jr., and Carolyn B. Neault. *By the Flow of the Inland River*. N.p., n.d.

P'Pool, Kenneth H. "The Architectural History of a Mississippi Town 1817-1866." 1990.

GREENWOOD

Smith, Frank E. *The Yazoo River*. 1954. Reprint, Jackson: University Press of Mississippi, 1988.

Williams Landing/Carroll County. Williams Landing Sesquicentennial, 1983.

HATTIESBURG

McCarty, Kenneth G., Jr., ed. *Hattiesburg: A Pictorial History*. Hattiesburg: Woodland Enterprises, 1989.

McMurtrey, Linda. "Historic Hattiesburg: History and Architecture of Hattiesburg's First Neighborhoods." Hattiesburg: City of Hattiesburg, Dept. of Planning and Community Development, undated.

HOLLY SPRINGS

Miller, Mary Carol. *Marshall County: From the Collection of Chesley Thorne Smith*. Charleston: Arcadia Press, 1998.

McAlexander, Hubert H. "Flush Times in Holly Springs." *Journal of Mississippi History* 48 (February 1986).

Smith, Chesley T. *Childhood in Holly Springs*. Lafayette, California: Berryhill Press, 1996.

Winter, Milton Robert. *Shadow of A Mighty Rock*. Franklin, Tennessee: Providence House, 1997.

Wyatt, Mary Eleanor. "The Depot and Related Areas of Holly Springs, Mississippi." Unpublished manuscript.

continued

JACKSON

Brinson, Carroll. *Jackson: A Special Kind of Place*. Jackson, 1977.

Cain, Helen and Anne D. Czarniecki. *An Illustrated Guide to the Mississippi Governor's Mansion*. Jackson: University Press of Mississippi, 1984.

Greaves, Linda Thompson, et. al. ed., *Jackson Landmarks*. Jackson: Calvin Hale Advertising, 1982.

McLemore, Carl. *Jackson: The Way We Were*. N.p., n.d.

Sansing, David G. and Carroll Waller. *A History of the Mississippi Governor's Mansion*. Jackson: University Press of Mississippi, 1977.

Skates, John Ray. *Mississippi's Old Capitol: Biography of a Building*. Jackson: Mississippi Department of Archives and History, 1990.

MERIDIAN

Fairley, Laura Nan and James T. Dawson. *Meridian: Paths to the Past*. Meridian: Lauderdale Department of Archives and History, 1988.

Turitz, Leo E. and Evelyn Turitz. *Jews in Early Mississippi*. Jackson: University Press of Mississippi, 1995.

NATCHEZ

Davis, Edwin Adams, and William Ransom Hogan. *The Barber of Natchez*. Baton Rouge: LSU Press, 1973.

James, D. Clayton. *Antebellum Natchez*. 1968. Reprint, Baton Rouge: LSU Press, 1993.

Kane, Harnett T. *Natchez on the Mississippi*. New York: William Morrow and Company, 1947.

Miller, Mary Warren, Ronald W. Miller and David King Gleason. *The Great Houses of Natchez*. Jackson: University Press of Mississippi, 1986.

Polk, Noel, ed. *Natchez Before 1830*. Jackson: University Press of Mississippi, 1989.

Sansing, David G., Sim C. Callon and Carolyn Vance Smith. *Natchez: An Illustrated History*. Natchez: Plantation Publishing Company, 1992.

Whitwell, William L. *The Heritage of Longwood*. Jackson: University Press of Mississippi, 1975.

OCEAN SPRINGS

Along the Gulf, 1895. Reprint: Pass Christian Historical Society, 1971.

Bellande, Ray. "Souse les chenes" columns in *Ocean Springs Record*.

Schmidt, C.E. *Ocean Springs: French Beachhead*. Pascagoula: Lewis Printing, 1972.

OXFORD

Crews, John. "A Goodly Heritage." Undated manuscript.

Miner, Ward. *The World of William Faulkner*. New York: Pageant Book Company, 1959.

Sansing, David. *Making Haste Slowly: The Troubled History of Higher Education in Mississippi*. Jackson: University Press of Mississippi, 1990.

Sobotka, John C. *A History of Lafayette County, Mississippi*. Oxford: Rebel Press, 1976.

Taylor, Herman E. *Faulkner's Oxford: Recollections and Reflections*. Nashville: Rutledge Hill Press, 1990.

Wilson, Jack Case. *Faulkners, Fortunes and Flames*. Nashville: Annandale Press, 1984.

PASS CHRISTIAN

Caire, Ronny and Katy Caire. *History of Pass Christian*. Pass Christian: 1976.

Ellis, Dan. *Pass Christian Tri-Centennial*. N.p., 1997.

Along the Gulf, 1895. Reprint: Pass Christian Historical Society, 1971.

Oliver, Nola Nance. *The Gulf Coast of Mississippi*. New York: Hastings House, 1941.

TUPELO

Grisham, Vaughn L., Jr.. "Tupelo, Mississippi, from Settlement to Industrial Community." Doctoral Dissertation, University of North Carolina, 1975.

Ramage, Martis D., ed. *Tupelo, 1911*. Reprint, Tupelo: Northeast Mississippi Historical and Genealogical Society, 1994.

—. *The Tupelo Tornado of 1936*. Tupelo: Northeast Mississippi Historical Genealogical Society, 1996.

Napoli, Olivia. *Grit, Greed and Guts*. N.p., 1980.

Northeast Mississippi Daily Journal 125th Anniversary Edition, May 21, 1995.

VICKSBURG

Harrell, Virginia C. *Vicksburg and the River*. Vicksburg: Harrell Publications, 1986.

Cotton, Gordon. *The Old Courthouse*. Raymond: Keith Printing Company, 1982.

—. *Vicksburg: Southern Stories of the Siege*. N.p., 1988.

YAZOO CITY

Bull, Susie. "General and Mrs. Benjamin Sherrod Ricks, Contributors to Business, Education and Culture." Unpublished manuscript in Ricks Memorial Library, 1973.

Olden, Sam. "Yazoo Historical Society" columns in *Yazoo Herald*.

Prichard, JoAnne and Harriet DeCell. *Yazoo: Its Legends and Legacies*. Yazoo City: Yazoo Delta Press, 1976.

Index